D0616904

Especially for

_____

From

_____

Date

_____

Published by Barbour Publishing, Inc., P.O. Box 719, Uhrichsville, Ohio 44683, www.barbourbooks.com

Our mission is to publish and distribute inspirational products offering exceptional value and biblical encouragement to the masses.

Printed in China.

Refreshment for the
Body and Soul

Spa-*"aah"*

Moments *for* Women

Donna K. Maltese

BARBOUR
PUBLISHING

Welcome to Spa-"aah" Moments for Women.

These one-minute devotional readings focus on your spiritual and emotional needs, offering a quick rejuvenation of mind, body, spirit, and soul—whether you're at home or work, running errands, or relaxing in the tub. Each entry is brief enough for the busiest woman and includes a relevant scripture passage, prayer, and "spa moment" tip—ways to relax and/or improve your life. This little book will give you just the boost of inspiration you need to meet the daily challenges on your journey. Ready for spiritual renewal? Set to take on a new attitude? Begin!

Simply Marvelous!

Thank you for making me so wonderfully complex!
Your workmanship is marvelous—how well I know it.
PSALM 139:14 NLT

God thinks you're perfect as you are. He adores you, and He wants you to know just how much. On days when you're feeling down and need a boost of assurance, remember not only who you are—but *whose* you are. You belong to the King!

Father God, thank You for the fine job You did in making me

Spa-"aah" Moment!

Buy an inexpensive bouquet of flowers. Split them up so you have at least one flower in every room of the house. The simplicity of a fresh bloom will brighten your home and your spirit.

Renewable You!

*Those who hope in the L*ORD
will renew their strength.
They will soar on wings like eagles;
they will run and not grow weary,
they will walk and not be faint.
ISAIAH 40:31

Solar energy is the new green. But it's got nothing on God, the original and mightiest power source we have. Need to be recharged? Put your hope in God. Plug into His promises. He'll give you the strength you need to do the impossible.

Lord, I need a boost of energy. Fill me with Your power so that I can soar like the eagle.

Spa "aah" Moment!

Light a scented candle. Then close your eyes and imagine God filling your entire being with His strength. In doing so, you will feel spiritually and physically recharged, ready to walk tall and face any challenge.

Inner Quiet

*I have composed and quieted my soul;
like a weaned child rests against his mother,
my soul is like a weaned child within me.*
PSALM 131:2 NASB

The things of this world cannot satisfy. But God can. Let Him wean you from your worldly desires. Like a little baby, crawl up onto Abba God's lap. Breathe deeply. Basking in His presence, your soul will find rest.

Abba God, take me in Your arms. Hold me tight. Fill me with Your comforting peace.

Spa-"aah" Moment!

Buy a sprig of baby's breath and place it where you spend most of your time. It will remind you that in God's eyes, we are mere infants. It's okay to run into His arms to find peace and rest. He's waiting.

Untold Blessings

"For I know the plans I have for you," declares the LORD,
"plans to prosper you and not to harm you, plans to
give you hope and a future."
JEREMIAH 29:11

Although your plans may not succeed, God's will. Unlike today's financial institutions, you can "bank" on God with assurance. He's got your life plan all worked out. Whew! What a relief!

I'm not sure what the future holds, Lord, but I trust Your plans and await Your blessings.

Spa-"aah" Moment!

Make a list of how God has blessed you today. If you do this daily, you'll be amazed, filled with infinite joy at how much He's taken care of you!

Walk Bold

"Be strong and of good courage; do not be afraid, nor be dismayed,
for the LORD your God is with you wherever you go."
JOSHUA 1:9 NKJV

God gives you strength and courage to face anything and everything. With Him, you can boldly go where no woman has gone before! Whenever fear creeps into your mind, say the above verse aloud and watch your doubts crumble before the presence of God!

Thank You, Lord, for Your strength and encouragement. I am Your emboldened woman! Hear me roar!

Spa "aah" Moment!

With God on your side, fears and discouragements tumble like dominoes. Carry a domino around with you until you have Joshua 1:9 memorized. Then whenever you feel afraid, remember this verse and watch your anxieties topple!

Satisfaction Guaranteed

I have learned how to be content with whatever I have.
PHILIPPIANS 4:11 NLT

God has promised to provide for you. There's no need to pine for what you do not have, but rather find delight in what you *do* have! For it's in the simple things in life that you will find the most joy.

As my Father, Lord, You have supplied me with all I need. Thank You—for everything!

Spa-"aah" Moment!

Enjoy watching the sun rise or set, or the clouds, moon, and stars as they roll across the sky. These are free and simple gifts the Father of lights bestows upon you. And they are beyond price!

Fill 'er Up!

In returning [to Me] and resting [in Me] you shall be saved;
in quietness and in [trusting] confidence shall be your strength.
ISAIAH 30:15 AMP

When you are frazzled, anxious, and stressed, you are disconnected to the force that is yours for the taking—the power of God. Return to Him and rest in Him. Amid the quiet, your confidence in Him will grow, and your strength will be restored!

I return to and rest in You, O God, confident that I am being renewed with Your strength.

Spa-"aah" Moment!

Find a quiet and safe place to lie down. Close your eyes and breathe deeply. As you reconnect with God, believe that He is increasing your strength. You will arise refreshed, restored, and resilient. May His force be with you!

Great Expectations

My soul, wait thou only upon God;
for my expectation is from him.
PSALM 62:5 KJV

The one thing you can count on is God. Simply have patience, confident He will do as promised. Go out today with assurance, expecting good things from the Lord; in doing so, you'll find your cup runneth over!

I wait upon You only, God. My hands are open, waiting to receive!

Spa-"aah" Moment!

When you take a shower today, cup your hands, letting them overflow with water. That's how much God is going to bless your life! *Aah*—how refreshingly sweet He is!

Blessings of Faith

Now faith is the substance of things hoped for,
the evidence of things not seen.
HEBREWS 11:1 NKJV

Exercise your faith today, believing that, regardless of what you observe in the material world, the desires of your heart will be fulfilled. There's no doubt about it; God is working in unseen ways. Blessed are you who believe!

Lord, You are working in my life, giving it substance. And I praise You for it!

Spa-"aah" Moment!

Take a few moments to watch the wind, a force that exists, although it is invisible. Allow the wind to remind you of God—unseen, yet He *is* and is everywhere!

Sweet Direction

Whoever gives heed to instruction prospers,
and blessed is the one who trusts in the LORD.
PROVERBS 16:20

Sometimes only when all else fails do we read the instructions. Before walking out the door, find inspiration and direction from scripture. Then trust in God's guidance, and you will prosper as promised!

Thank You, Lord, for Your Guidebook and helping me to walk Your way.

Spa-"aah" Moment!

Bake one of your favorite desserts. When it cools, take a bite and think about how you couldn't have made it without following the instructions. Imagine what sweet things God has in store for you when you follow His Manual!

Looking Forward

> "Escape for your life! Do not look behind you. . . ."
> But [Lot's] wife, from behind him, looked back,
> and she became a pillar of salt.
> GENESIS 19:17, 26 NASB

God is here to help you escape for your life. So, instead of lamenting past decisions, choices, and hurts, move forward, knowing God is leading you to greater opportunities!

Lord, help me move forward, knowing You are with me every step of the way and that better days await me!

Spa-"aah" Moment!

Try walking forward while looking behind you. You can't do it without stumbling, right? Now walk facing forward and pay attention to what's around you. A new opportunity lies ahead. Look for it!

Metamorphosis

Be not conformed to this world: but be ye transformed
by the renewing of your mind.
ROMANS 12:2 KJV

Reprogram your mind daily, replacing worldly negatives with spiritual positives. By putting on a new attitude, you'll change your latitude!

Fill my mind with the goodness of Your Word, Lord. Keep my heart, mind, soul, and spirit focused on You as I step out into the world.

Spa-"aah" Moment!

Tonight, pull yourself away from the TV and snuggle up with the Bible or another good inspirational book. You'll find your mind refreshed and your spirit lifted! It's a win-win for your inner and outer being!

Miracle Ear

*Whether you turn to the right or to the left, your ears will hear
a voice behind you, saying, "This is the way; walk in it."*
ISAIAH 30:21

Keep your ears open, listening attentively for God to speak
to you. He'll let you know which way to go—and give you
the power to walk that path! Listen—then step out in faith!

*I don't need a miracle ear to hear You, Lord. I just need to keep
myself open to Your voice. Speak to me, Lord! I'm listening!*

Spa-"aah" Moment!

Take some time to sit outside. Open your ears to the
sounds around you, and revel in the knowledge that
God, as well as His creation, is speaking to you. All you
need to do is stop—and listen.

Unloading Zone

Cast your burden on the Lord [releasing the weight of it]
and He will sustain you.
PSALM 55:22 AMP

Plagued by stooped shoulders? Get into the God Zone and unload your burden. He's strong enough to take it *and* hold you up at the same time—thank God!

I feel so weighed down, Lord. Here (umph!) is my burden. Whew! Thanks for taking on my load! Now I'm freed up to take on the challenges of this day! Thank You, God!

Spa-"aah" Moment!

Find an old suitcase. Write down all your troubles, pack them away, and imagine God picking up your baggage. Then give Him a praise tip and go on your merry way!

Daughters of the King

> Yet some people accepted him
> and put their faith in him.
> So he gave them the right
> to be the children of God.
> JOHN 1:12 CEV

Jesus is the King of kings! That makes you—a child of God—a princess! Embrace that sense of royalty, and claim the privileges and power that come with it!

Thank You, Abba God, for adopting me! I am regenerated in You!

Spa-"aah" Moment!

You're royalty, so pamper yourself today with a nice bubble bath. Nothing buoys your spirit more than a tubful of water!

21

Above the Fray

God is our refuge and strength, a very present help in trouble.
PSALM 46:1 KJV

God is the one constant, the one thing you can count on to shield you from trouble. Put your hand in His, and allow Him to lift you above the fray. He won't let you fall!

Lord, You are my safe haven. As I abide in You today, fill me with Your strength.

Spa-"aah" Moment!

Rest your open hand on your lap. Now close your eyes, and imagine God taking your hand and lifting you up out of all your troubles. As you go through the day, know that God is still holding your hand and will never let go.

The Key

*Trust in the LORD with all your heart
and lean not on your own understanding.*
PROVERBS 3:5

The key to a worry-free life is to accept the fact that you'll never comprehend it all. But that's okay. You don't have to. God's got you covered. Just trust in Him.

*Lord, although I don't always understand why things happen,
I know I can rely on You.*

Spa-"aah" Moment!

Plant a tree. Although you may not understand exactly how a seed becomes a huge tree or how trees reduce your carbon footprint, you don't need to. Rest in the knowledge that God has it all under control.

Getting into Focus

*I focus on this one thing: Forgetting the past
and looking forward to what lies ahead.*
PHILIPPIANS 3:13 NLT

There are days when past hurts and grievances hold you
down from experiencing the life God has planned for you.
Break free from those ties, and fix your eyes on opportunities ahead! God has the plan all worked out. All you have
to do is move forward!

*I'm cutting the ties that bind today, Lord! Help me to refocus
on You and Your will for my life!*

Spa-"aah" Moment!

Write a list of things you'd like to accomplish. Then
spend time visualizing them every day, anticipating the
moment when your dreams become a reality!

Mmmm, Lifesavers!

*"Come to me with your ears wide open.
Listen, and you will find life."*
ISAIAH 55:3 NLT

God's Word is filled with lifesavers. How sweet they are! All you need to do is read His Word, listen for His message within, and put His to-do plan into action. Soon you'll find yourself living the abundant life!

I'm opening myself up to You and Your Word, Lord. Show me how to live!

Spa-"aah" Moment!

Buy yourself a roll of Lifesavers, then, over time, slowly savor each one, remembering that God's Word is sweeter than honey. And it's good to "eat" a little every day!

Supreme Makeover

Create in me a clean heart, O God;
and renew a right spirit within me.
PSALM 51:10 KJV

God has the power to renew your heart and spirit. All you have to do is ask Him! And He'll give you the supreme spiritual makeover, leaving you refreshed, replenished, and rejuvenated! *Aah*, that feels good!

Lord, thank You for making me beautiful—within and without.

Spa-"aah" Moment!

Treat yourself to an appointment at your local beauty parlor. As you get your manicure, pedicure, or (*eek!*) waxing, ask God to give you an internal makeover. Next thing you know, you'll be sitting pretty—inside and out!

The Victory Is Yours!

We are more than conquerors through Him who loved us.
ROMANS 8:37 NKJV

No matter what happens in the physical world, you will never be defeated. Nothing can keep you from God's love. It will always be with you, pulling you up off the mat and into victory—day after day after day!

I am amazed at Your unfailing love, Lord. It's more powerful than a locomotive!

Spa-"aah" Moment!

Treat yourself to some downtime by watching a super-hero movie, remembering that, with God in your life, you are a superwoman! With His power, you can leap tall troubles in a single bound! You go, girl!

To-Dos and Ta-Das

The LORD my God will help you do everything needed.
1 CHRONICLES 28:20 CEV

At times the list of tasks before you may seem overwhelming. You wonder how you'll ever get them all done. Relax. Take heart. God will give you the strength to do whatever needs to be done today. The rest can wait till tomorrow.

I put my day in Your hands, Lord. Guide me in prioritizing my tasks.

Spa-"aah" Moment!

When you complete a task, be sure to check it off your list. Recognizing a "ta-da!" after each "to-do" is done will give you a sense of satisfaction and accomplishment!

Just Do It!

Be strong and of good courage, and do it:
fear not, nor be dismayed.
1 CHRONICLES 28:20 KJV

Nothing builds confidence more than knowing God is in your corner as you step out into the world. Just have faith that He is with you, directing your day. Take courage. There's nothing you will face that He can't handle. Just do it!

Thank You, God, for giving me the courage to face any challenge that comes my way.

Spa-"aah" Moment!

Throughout your day, imagine God being by your side, surrounding you with His protection, light, love, strength, and courage. Doing so will boost your confidence and fill you with empowerment.

An Unstoppable Force!

"Whoever believes in me. . .rivers of living water will flow from within them."
JOHN 7:38

Moving water has the power to shape rocks, mountains, and valleys. Christ within you is a continual, unstoppable force of living water, molding you, feeding you, directing you, flushing out your doubts and fears, and putting a spring of joy in your step!

Jesus, quench my thirst. Fill me with Your living water.

Spa-"aah" Moment!

Whenever you take a drink of water today, remember the living water that lies within you. Then allow Christ's power and love to flow out of you and into the lives of those you meet. You can change their world!

Winging It!

"May you be richly rewarded by the LORD. . .under whose wings you have come to take refuge."
RUTH 2:12

When you feel bruised, beaten, and battered by the world, run to the Lord. He will give you shelter under His wings, mend your wounds, and give you rest. As you abide in Him, you will find peace, comfort, and rewards uncountable.

Lord, I run to You today. I thank You for making me whole again!

Spa-"aah" Moment!

Pick up some birdseed and either scatter it upon your lawn or refill your bird feeder. As you watch the birds gather, remember that God's wings are stretched out, just waiting to shelter you.

Mission Possible!

I can do all things through Him who strengthens me.
PHILIPPIANS 4:13 NASB

There is nothing—absolutely nothing—you cannot do! There is no "mission impossible" when you are working through Christ. The possibilities are endless! Your potential limitless. Christ has already given you the boundless power and strength to succeed!

With You, Lord, I can do anything. Let's go!

Spa-"aah" Moment!

Spend some time daydreaming about what you want to be or do. Then, with Philippians 4:13 written on your heart, acknowledge God's limitless power and strength working in you, and set out to make your dreams come true!

Keeping Cool

The LORD himself watches over you!
The LORD stands beside you as your protective shade.
PSALM 121:5 NLT

In these days when the sun's rays can be lethal, you need to be careful not to get burned. Consider our Super Beneficent Father (SBF) as your ultimate protection. With Him standing beside you, you have it made in the shade. How cool is that?

Thank You for protecting me, Lord, no matter where I am.

Spa-"aah" Moment!

Lather yourself up in suntan lotion, throw a beach chair and a good book in your car, and head for the nearest park. Then spend some time reading or napping in the sun. It's a great pick-me-up!

GodQuest

You wisely and tenderly lead me,
and then you bless me.
PSALM 73:24 MSG

When you need direction, MapQuest has nothing on GodQuest. Simply click on GodQuest (pray), and check out the road map (your Bible). When you get your directions, take the path God has chosen for you. He will lead you to blessings untold.

I need Your direction, Lord. Show me the way through Your Word.

Spa-"aah" Moment!

Grab a road map and take a trip to somewhere you've never been before, whether it be another town, county, or state. A change of scenery will give you a new perspective.

Disarming Truth

"You will not have to fight this battle. Take up your positions; stand firm and see the deliverance the LORD will give you. . . . Do not be afraid."
2 CHRONICLES 20:17

Our undefeatable God, the Doer of amazing things, is ready to fight your battle and keep you safe in the midst of conflict. All you need to do is stand firm and praise Him, claiming victory in His name! Now that's faith! And it works miracles!

I know the victory is Yours, Lord, and I praise Your name!

Spa-"aah" Moment!

Did you know you burn more calories standing up than sitting? Whenever you have an opportunity, stand while talking on the phone. Trade phone calls with walks over to the neighbor. Don't just sit there—stand!

"Son-shine"

In him we live, and move, and have our being.
ACTS 17:28 KJV

It's a new day in which God has given you breath and life! Relish the days He gives you! Take the opportunities He affords you! Cherish the love He has bestowed upon you, and share it with others! Go forward and shine in the Son!

Lord, thank You for the gift of life and breath!

Spa-"aah" Moment!

Lean back in the sunlight. Relax, allowing the rays to warm your body. Breathe in and out slowly three times while whispering, "Jesus," on each exhale. Then rise and spread your "Son-shine"!

The "Go-To" Guy

I sought the LORD, and he heard me,
and delivered me from all my fears.
PSALM 34:4 KJV

When you need courage, there's only one go-to guy—
God! Not only will He *hear* you, but He'll also *help* you
by banishing your fears. And not only will He work on the
inside, by quieting your soul, but He'll also work on the
outside, defeating your foes. What victory!

Beloved Lord, hear my prayer. Vanquish my fears and revive
my spirit.

Spa-"aah" Moment!

Spread God's light by performing a random act of kindness today for an unsuspecting stranger. Perhaps you will
find that you are the answer to someone else's prayer.
Oh, what a feeling!

Streams of Peace

You keep him in perfect peace
whose mind is stayed on you,
because he trusts in you.
ISAIAH 26:3 ESV

When your eyes are on God, everything else fades into gray—problems seem smaller, foes weaker, and sorrows dimmer. With the All-Powerful God the only thing in view, you will experience a peace beyond all understanding.

I trust in You, Lord, and feel Your heavenly peace in the eye of this storm.

Spa-"aah" Moment!

Take a physical or mental walk to a stream. Close your eyes, and listen to the water as it flows across the rocks. Take deep breaths, and imagine God's spirit flowing over you and in you. *Aah. . .*what peace!

Relief!

"Come to me, all you who are weary and burdened,
and I will give you rest."
MATTHEW 11:28

The burdens of life can make you overanxious, over-
weight, and overwrought. What's a woman to do? Go to
Jesus. Take the burdens off, one by one, leave them at His
feet, and resist the temptation to pick them up again! *Aah,*
that's a relief!

Lord, here is what's been weighing me down. Please. . .take it—
and keep it!

Spa-"aah" Moment!

Grab some paper and spend a few moments writing down
the things troubling you. Next, pray, turning each problem over to Jesus. Then destroy the list, for your troubles
are now in His hands. You can meet the day, unfettered.

The New You

"The Spirit of the LORD will come powerfully upon you. . .
and you will be changed into a different person."
1 SAMUEL 10:6

It's hard when you are working in your own power. What
you need is to recognize the power of God's Spirit working within you. When you get attuned to the Spirit, He
can do amazing things in, through, and with you. When
you let go and let God, astonishing things happen!

Holy Spirit, I'm ready to step aside! Come shining through!

Spa-"aah" Moment!

Turn on a light. Notice how it comes on immediately
because it's plugged into the power source. Now imagine plugging yourself into the ultimate source—God's
Spirit—and shine, shine, shine!

A Four-in-One Workout

*I will sing the LORD's, praise
for he has been good to me.*
PSALM 13:6

Singing is good for you in so many ways. Physically, it exercises your lungs and heart. Emotionally, it lifts your spirits. It also benefits you mentally and spiritually. So, don't be shy. Belt out a tune, and give yourself a four-in-one workout!

Lord, I will sing my praises to You! Ready?

Spa-"aah" Moment!

Learn the words and music to a praise song that touches your heart. Then sing out! Even if you can't carry a tune, God doesn't care. Your singing is sweet to His ears and reaps benefits galore!

Beyond Your Imagination

Now all glory to God, who is able, through his mighty power at work within us, to accomplish infinitely more than we might ask or think.
EPHESIANS 3:20 NLT

The things you can do when God is working through you are beyond your imagination. So don't limit yourself. Tap into His infinite power, connect to His Spirit, and let Him take the reins on your life. The results will be awesome!

God, I stand at the ready. Work through me!

Spa-"aah" Moment!

Open your mind and heart to the will of God. Allow Him to whisper His ideas in your ears. Then walk assured He will equip you for the work ahead! And give Him all the glory.

One Sure Thing

"LORD, there is no one besides You to help in the battle between the powerful and those who have no strength."
2 CHRONICLES 14:11 NASB

God is the one sure thing you can count on in this life. Riches, people, and possessions may fail you, but God never will. Face life with assurance that when you are weak, He is your strength. He'll fight your battles for you!

Thank You, God, for taking this battle into Your hands!

Spa-"aah" Moment!

Find a place in your house that can serve as your prayer nook. If possible, decorate it with things that will help you focus on seeking the Lord. Then spend time there, putting your battles into His hands.

Opportunity Knocking

*"Yet who knows whether you have come to
the kingdom for such a time as this?"*
ESTHER 4:14 NKJV

Wherever God has placed you is the place where He wants
you to be. Your job is to find out what you can do there to
accomplish His purpose for this generation. Opportunities
await you. Seek them out, and watch untold miracles
unfold!

I thank You for this opportunity, Lord. Show me what to do!

Spa-"aah" Moment!

Keep your eyes open, alert to opportunities God has
placed in your path. Then go forward to serve Him, even
if it's out of your comfort zone. Don't let your chance
slip through your fingers!

Pray!

*"Ask, and it will be given to you; seek, and you will find;
knock, and it will be opened to you."*
MATTHEW 7:7 NASB

Looking for direction? Pray. God's door is always open.
He'll give you the answers, help you find what you're looking for, and provide you with opportunities when you
knock. Don't just sit there! Pray!

Father God, here I am—asking, seeking, knocking.

Spa-"aah" Moment!

Take a nice long walk in your neighborhood. As you pass
each house or business, say a little prayer asking God to
bless those who reside or work there. By the time you get
home, your soul and body will be lighter!

"I Believe!"

When you ask for something, you must have faith and not doubt.
JAMES 1:6 CEV

It's one thing to pray for something. It's another to believe you'll get it. Once you ask, trust that God will bring it to pass. Do not waver. Do not doubt. Keep your heart and mind united, and God will turn your requests into reality!

Lord, I believe! My heart and mind are one!

Spa-"aah" Moment!

Think of some situation that is challenging you right now. Bring it to God, knowing He can do the impossible. Replace your "we'll see" attitude with the statement "I believe God will make a way where there seems to be no way." Then expect your prayer to be answered!

The Whys

"I know that you can do all things;
no purpose of yours can be thwarted."
JOB 42:2

Sometimes what you think should happen doesn't. But rest assured, God has a great plan for your life. All you need to do is let Him work it out. He can turn ashes into beauty. What a wonderful God you have!

I have so many "whys" on my lips. But I know, Lord, that You will somehow work this out for my good. And I praise You for that!

Spa-"aah" Moment!

Get a new perspective by spending some time with children. You may not be able to answer all the "why" questions they ask, but you can tell them that Father God has it all under control!

Do Not Disturb

Meditate within your heart on your bed, and be still.
PSALM 4:4 NKJV

The demands you have on your life can sometimes make you feel like there aren't enough hours in the day. Perhaps it's time to be still. Rest. Afterward, you will rise with a calmer heart and mind, refreshed and renewed. *Aah*, that's better!

Lord, hold me in Your arms as I rest in You.

Spa-"aah" Moment!

Find some time to catch up on your sleep. Put a Do Not Disturb sign on your bedroom door if you have to. Then, when you awaken, continue to lie still in bed. It'll do your body, mind, and spirit good!

Take Heart

The LORD will work out his plans for my life—
for your faithful love, O LORD, endures forever.
PSALM 138:8 NLT

When all seems lost, when goals seem unattainable, when you feel unloved, do not despair! God is working things out! After all, He loves you! So take heart, woman. You've got the Supreme Being on *your* side!

Lord, thank You for loving me!

Spa-"aah" Moment!

Share God's adoration of you by doing a favor for someone else today. Keep your eyes open. There's someone out there who really needs a touch of His—and your—love!

Foot in Mouth

The LORD will be your confidence
and will keep your foot from being caught.
PROVERBS 3:26 ESV

Ah, the temptations that you face. The things you long to say. Careful. Before you speak, mentally run your words by God. You can trust Him to keep you from catching foot-in-mouth disease.

God, keep an eye (and ear) on my words today!

Spa-"aah" Moment!

Be a builder-upper today. Speak only those things that edify, confident that God is listening. You'll be amazed at how good it feels when you are boosting others!

Steady There, Girl

"Be careful, keep calm and don't be afraid. Do not lose heart."
ISAIAH 7:4

Never worry. Never fear. No matter what you are up against, God is with you. So keep calm and steady. Put one foot in front of the other. And trust God to see you safely through. He's fought tougher battles than this!

I'm trusting You, Lord, to see me through.

Spa-"aah" Moment!

Spend at least five minutes today (and every day) taking deep breaths. It's not only relaxing, but it's also a good exercise for your lungs, builds up your immune system, and filters out toxins. *Aah*, fresh air!

You Called?

Lead a life worthy of your calling,
for you have been called by God.
EPHESIANS 4:1 NLT

To live a worthy life, do what God has called you to do. What does your heart urge you toward? What would God approve of you doing? Where do your talents lie? That is your calling. Now go! Do!

Lord, I want to live a worthy life for You!

Spa-"aah" Moment!

Spend some time daydreaming. If you could do anything in the world, what would it be? Forget about obstacles. Let your imagination run wild. When you have an idea of your calling, talk to God about it. He'll send you in the right direction!

Peace Rains

"I leave you peace; my peace I give you. . . .
So don't let your hearts be troubled or afraid."
JOHN 14:27 NCV

No wonder the angels were excited when Jesus was born.
He came to give humankind peace like no other. All *you*
have to do to obtain His peace is commune with God.
With that peace upon you, fret and fear disappear! Peace,
sister, peace!

Jesus, rain Your peace upon me!

Spa-"aah" Moment!

Sit outside in a safe place the next time it rains. Listen to
the drops as they fall upon the ground. Close your eyes,
and imagine the peace of Jesus raining upon you in the
same way. It'll cool you off in more ways than one!

Rich in Deed

"Do to others as you would like them to do to you."
LUKE 6:31 NLT

What a wonderful world this would be if everyone treated others like they'd want to be treated. Such a movement can become a reality though. And it can begin with you. Follow this Golden Rule, and you will be rich indeed!

Help me follow Your Golden Rule, Lord!

Spa-"aah" Moment!

Find an opportunity to do a good deed. Try paying the toll for the car behind you. Or give the grocery-store cashier some money for the person behind you in the checkout line. There's a million ways to share the riches found in the Golden Rule!

Powder Protection

Lord, you bless those who do what is right.
Like a shield, your loving care keeps them safe.
PSALM 5:12 NIrV

Sometimes it's hard to do the right thing. But the upside is that when you do what's right, you're blessed with God's love and protection. No sticks and stones can break your spiritual bones. Not when you walk forward in God's name!

Thank You, God, for Your care and protection.

Spa-"aah" Moment!

After your shower, treat yourself to scented powder. As you apply it to your body, remember that God's love is protecting your soul like the powder is protecting your skin. The difference is that God's love will never wash off!

Good to Go

For the Spirit God gave us does not make us timid,
but gives us power, love and self-discipline.
2 TIMOTHY 1:7

The Holy Spirit gives you all the resources you need to overcome fear. So tap into His inexhaustible power for courage. Allow your banner of love for God to lift you above the fear of man. And, lastly, discipline your mind to trust Him. You're unbeatable!

Thank You, God, for Your Holy Spirit. I'm good to go!

Spa-"aah" Moment!

Challenge yourself by doing something new, like learning how to play the guitar, speak another language, or dance. Pluck up your courage and dive right in. And go, go, go for God!

He Is Here!

*"I am God and not a human.
I'm The Holy One and I'm here—in your very midst."*
HOSEA 11:9 MSG

God is not human. He will not carry a grudge. He is not imperfect. He will not leave you. He is holy and He is right here—in your midst! Just reach out and touch Him. Talk to Him. Seek Him out. Feel His presence. He is here! Hallelujah!

You are with me wherever I go, Lord! I praise Your name!

Spa-"aah" Moment!

Take yourself on a nature walk where you can enjoy the beauty that surrounds you. Then celebrate your life and God's presence by praising Him in the midst of His creation! That's a joyful noise!

Rah, Rah, Rah!

"Arise! For this matter is your responsibility,
but we will be with you; be courageous and act."
EZRA 10:4 NASB

Facing unexpected responsibility may fray the nerves. Fortunately, you can find the courage to act when others cheer you on and promise you support. And, remember, God is a permanent part of your rooting section. So be brave, and do what needs to be done!

Lord, I rise and act in Your strength!

Spa "aah" Moment!

Make a date to have lunch with a trusted friend. Perhaps she'll give you a new perspective on a problem or just the encouragement you need to take action.

Bad-News Bears

The Lord is a place of safety for those who have been beaten down.
He keeps them safe in times of trouble.
PSALM 9:9 NIrV

Today's news media seems to bear nothing but bad reports. It's enough to keep a good woman down—unless she makes a concerted effort to turn her thoughts, heart, and soul to God. With Him, you are safe. Let Him lift you above the world's chaos.

Beam me up, God. Lift me above this world's turmoil.

Spa-"aah" Moment!

For the next few days, try to avoid news broadcasts. A break from the headlines may be just the thing to lift your soul, recharge your spirit, and change your outlook.

Heart in Hand

"You will seek me and find me,
when you seek me with all your heart."
JEREMIAH 29:13 ESV

When people feel far from God, it's not He who has moved; they have. He is never more than a cry away. When you come near to Him, whole heart in hand, He will be near to you. It's as simple as that.

Here I come, Lord. I lift myself heart and soul to you!

Spa-"aah" Moment!

For an untroubled night's sleep, imagine Jesus sitting in a chair right next to your bed, watching over you and lifting the burdens off you, one by one. Before you know it, you'll be in dreamland.

Armor All

Put on the full armor of God, so that. . .you may be able to stand your ground, and after you have done everything, to stand.
EPHESIANS 6:13

When you're standing in God's full armor, nothing can harm you. It's the ultimate protection. Shielded by faith, you will be able to face any danger. Stand firm and strong in this surety: God's got you covered!

With all Your armor covering me, I can stand up to anything. Thank You, God!

Spa "aah" Moment!

Treat yourself to a trip to a renaissance fair. Getting an up-close-and-personal look at knights in full armor will give you a new appreciation for God's protection!

Power Surge

*May [God] give you the power to accomplish all
the good things your faith prompts you to do.*
2 Thessalonians 1:11 nlt

God has already equipped you with the power to accomplish whatever your faith is calling you to do. What an awesome boost to your self-assurance. Start the day with this verse, and you will have confidence in everything! Walk tall, walk strong!

Lord, I walk confident that Your power is surging through me.

Spa-"aah" Moment!

Personalize this verse: "God is giving me the power to accomplish all the good things my faith prompts me to do." Then memorize it. When you make it your earnest and continuous prayer, amazing things will happen!

Broom Clean

Guard your heart above all else,
for it determines the course of your life.
PROVERBS 4:23 NLT

When you feel defeated, confused, or harassed, chances are you are letting negative thoughts overpower God's powerful, positive promises. Gird your mind with His truth. Your heart will soar, and your life will get back on the right course!

Help me guard my heart, God.

Spa-"aah" Moment!

Each morning, take an inventory of your thoughts. Imagine a broom sweeping away all the negative ones. Then replace them with positive verses from this devotional. They will freshen and beautify your newly clean "house" like a bouquet of flowers! Now that's heart smart!

Blessed beyond Compare

Without faith no one can please God. We must believe that God is real and that he rewards everyone who searches for him.
HEBREWS 11:6 CEV

God is just bursting to reward you with His forgiveness, power, strength, and mercy. All you have to do is believe that He *is* and keep seeking His presence. Continue to walk and talk with Him, and you will be blessed beyond compare!

I come into Your garden, Lord, ready to spend time in Your presence.

Spa-"aah" Moment!

Sit in a garden. Close your eyes, and imagine God seated on the bench beside you. Experience the joy you share as you linger there! What a rewarding experience!

Rescuer

"When my life was fainting away, I remembered the LORD,
and my prayer came to you, into your holy temple."
JONAH 2:7 ESV

Sometimes people do not seek God until they are in a deep pit of despair. But the cool thing is that God will listen to your prayer no matter how far you've fallen. Don't wait! Pray to God. He'll rescue you and forgive you, for you are precious in His sight!

Lord, lift me up into Your arms!

Spa-"aah" Moment!

Work on a new jigsaw puzzle to exercise your mind. When doing so, remember that although you're not sure how all the events in your life fit together, Father God sees the whole picture. So relax.

The God Signal

Since God is on our side, who can be against us?
ROMANS 8:31 NIrV

There's no need to quiver and shake. You have the ultimate Superhero on *your* side! No one can harm you, for God is bigger, stronger, and mightier than any foe you may face. Simply shine the God signal across the Gotham City of your mind. He'll be there in a flash!

How wonderful that with You in my life, Lord, nothing can prevail against me!

Spa-"aah" Moment!

Keep your eyes and ears open today for someone who needs some encouragement. You may have the words that person needs to hear, providing him or her with the strength to overcome.

Women Warriors

Let the weak say, I am strong [a warrior]!
JOEL 3:10 AMP

As a daughter of God, you have amazing resources at your fingertips. One of those assets is His strength. You need not be a worrier when God has equipped you to be a warrior. Let "I am strong" be your battle cry, and then watch God win the victory!

You are my stronghold, Lord! Victory is ours!

Spa-"aah" Moment!

Pick up a couple of light hand weights and begin some weight lifting. This type of exercise will help you reduce stress, increase your energy, and build stronger bones. And the only thing you'll lose is fat!

Raise in Praise

*"Only fear the LORD and serve him faithfully with all your heart.
For consider what great things he has done for you."*
1 SAMUEL 12:24 ESV

The Bible contains myriad accounts of the magnificent things God has done for His people. But He didn't stop there. God has done some amazing things in your own life and will continue to do so! What a wonderful God He is!

My heart belongs to You, Abba God. Thank You for working in my life!

Spa-"aah" Moment!

Take some time to go through an old photo album. As you do so, reflect upon where you have been, where you are today, and how God helped you in the past. Raise your voice in praise of His wondrous deeds!

Real Faith

*By faith Abraham, when called to go to a place he would
later receive as his inheritance, obeyed and went, even
though he did not know where he was going.*
HEBREWS 11:8

Real faith is stepping out into the unknown, willing to go
where God has called you even though you don't know
where you're headed. The great thing about it is that when
absolute faith moves people, God moves mountains.

I'm ready to go where You lead me, Lord.

Spa-"aah" Moment!

With no particular destination in mind, take a drive into
the country. Have faith that God is taking you where He
wants you to go. Then record what you encounter!

Cocooned in Love

"Neither fear them nor fear their words. . . .
Neither fear their words nor be dismayed at their presence."
EZEKIEL 2:6 NASB

At times, you may have to deal with difficult people, ones who say things that sting or wound your spirit. Fortunately, you have God's protection. When you abide in Christ's love, you need not fear. Be brave. Be bold. Believe. And all will be well.

Give me courage, Lord. Encase me in Your cocoon of love.

Spa-"aah" Moment!

Pray for someone who has wounded you with his or her words. Do so until you feel the peace of God transform your heart from bitter to benevolent. *That's* amazing grace!

Available 24-7

I praise the Lord because he advises me.
Even at night, I feel his leading.
PSALM 16:7 NCV

There's no need to let your troubles keep you awake. God provides guidance anytime, day or night. That means His wisdom is available 24-7. All you have to do is ask Him for it. Got a problem? Go to God! He's got all the answers.

Dear Abba, I need Your advice. Got a minute?

Spa-"aah" Moment!

Use scented sheet spray on your bedsheets. Lavender is known to help you relax—body, mind, soul, and spirit. Sweet dreams!

On Standby

They attacked me at a moment when I was in distress,
but the LORD supported me. He led me to a place of safety;
he rescued me because he delights in me.
PSALM 18:18–19 NLT

When you are at your lowest, you may be easy prey, open to attack. But not to worry. God is on standby, ready to lift you up out of trouble and set you down in a safe place. Why? Because He loves you! When you are weak, He is your strength!

Lord, thank You for always being there.

Spa-"aah" Moment!

When we run ourselves ragged, we're more open to distress and disease. This weekend, give yourself permission to sleep in. You deserve it!

From Here to Eternity

*[Jesus said,] "I came so they can have real and eternal life,
more and better life than they ever dreamed of."*
JOHN 10:10 MSG

Christ came to give you—yes, you!—an abundant life.
That includes salvation, healing, sustenance, and more!
More than you can ever dream or imagine. And that's from
here to eternity! You can't ask for anything better than that!

With You in my life, Jesus, I have everything I need and want.

Spa-"aah" Moment!

You have been blessed with an abundant life. That should
put a smile on your face. So show the world! Make it
a point today to smile at everyone you meet. You'll be
surprised and overjoyed by those who smile back.

Win-Win-Win

*"Well done, good and faithful servant! You have been faithful
with a few things; I will put you in charge of many things.
Come and share your master's happiness!"*
MATTHEW 25:21

When you use your talents, God rewards you for your
efforts, invites you to share in His joy, and gives you a
promotion to boot! It's a win-win-win. So unearth those
talents and go-go-go!

I am Your servant, Lord. Show me what You want me to do.

Spa-"aah" Moment!

Make a list of things you do well, and ask God which
ones He wants you to use in service to Him. Before you
know it, you'll get a sense of fulfillment you've never felt
before! How commendable!

Spirit Strength

*I am the LORD All-Powerful. So don't depend on
your own power or strength, but on my Spirit.*
ZECHARIAH 4:6 CEV

Exhausted from attempting things in your own strength?
Step aside and let God work through you. His Spirit has
the power to do *anything* through you. So rest easy, allow
God's Spirit to flow through you, and watch Him accomplish the impossible!

Work through me, Holy Spirit. I'm depending on You.

Spa-"aah" Moment!

Take a trip to an arts and crafts store. As you browse,
ask the Spirit what He'd like to do. Then purchase the
supplies, and give Him free rein to accomplish the task!
You'll be amazed at what you can do together.

One Constant

"I am the LORD, and I do not change."
MALACHI 3:6 NLT

In this world, change is the one thing you can count on. But God is not of this world. He is supernatural, other-worldly. And He *does not* change. His strength, saving grace, and power are a sure thing no matter where, no matter when. Count on it! Count on Him!

What a relief, God, that I can always depend on You.

Spa-"aah" Moment!

Over the next few weeks, collect all the spare change you can. Later, count it up, and use it to help pay for a movie or dinner out. Perhaps even treat a friend. See you there!

The New You

If anyone is in Christ, the new creation has come:
The old has gone, the new is here!
2 CORINTHIANS 5:17

With Christ in your life, you're a whole new you! You have a different spiritual and material perspective on life. You have a new attitude, one that is pleasing to God. Rejoice in your new life. That's what the angels in heaven are doing!

Lord, thank You for giving me new life in You!

Spa-"aah" Moment!

Give a room in your house a makeover by changing things up. Rearrange the furniture, and perhaps get some new pillows or wall hangings. Recognize that you've changed things inside—and out! Oh, what a feeling!

Muscle Woman

In your strength I can crush an army;
with my God I can scale any wall.
PSALM 18:29 NLT

God gives you the muscle to vanquish any foe and climb the highest walls. So, when you need a boost, remember you have an unseen power source fortifying you—body, mind, and soul. Claiming that promise, you can meet any challenge head-on.

I claim Your power, Lord. Help me overcome!

Spa-"aah" Moment!

Walking is one of the healthiest things you can do for your-self. Find some time today to take a brisk walk. If you can work yourself up to a thirty-minute-a-day walking routine, your body will strengthen, your mood will improve, and your weight will decrease. Now that's a challenge!

True Love

*I will always love you; that's why I've been so patient
and kind. You are precious to me.*
JEREMIAH 31:3–4 CEV

Nothin' says lovin' like God. His love for you is true. It's
of the everlasting kind. No matter what you do, God will
never stop loving you. Strong and powerful, His love is
unconditional. And you are His prized possession. What
sweet bliss!

*Lord, I don't know what I did to deserve Your love, but I
revel in it!*

Spa-"aah" Moment!

Spread God's love around by giving someone a hug today.
It'll make her day—and yours!

A Paradox

Whatever you ask for in prayer, believe (trust and be confident)
that it is granted to you, and you will [get it].
MARK 11:24 AMP

God doesn't want you to just ask Him for things. He wants you to *trust* Him to provide, to have confidence that He will deliver. So the formula is believe and receive! The cool thing is that the more you receive, the more you *will* believe. What an awesome paradox!

I believe, Jesus. I believe!

Spa-"aah" Moment!

Call your local food pantry, and find out what it needs. Then make a donation to replenish the cupboards. Who knows, you may find yourself being an answer to someone else's prayer. Sweet satisfaction!

Arrested Development

The LORD gives you rest from your sorrow, and from your fear.
ISAIAH 14:3 NKJV

When sorrow, pain, and fear develop within you, the Lord will give you His peace. All you need to do is reach out to Him. He'll give you the touch you need. By focusing your mind, heart, and soul on Him, your problems will recede. Got a minute? Get God.

Give me rest from my pain and sorrow, Lord. I need the peace found only in You.

Spa "aah" Moment!

Laughter is an amazing remedy. Take some time out of your day to watch a good sitcom or a romantic comedy. Doing so will lighten your load!

Food for the Journey

*The angel of the LORD came again a second time and touched him
and said, "Arise and eat, for the journey is too great for you."*
1 KINGS 19:7 ESV

God knows what's happening to you on your journey
through life. He is watching you, ready to encourage you
with whatever you need, whether it be spiritual or physical, rest or nourishment. He'll keep providing until you're
back on your feet.

Thank You, Lord, for coming to me when I need You.

Spa-"aah" Moment!

Try a new recipe at home tonight. Better yet, go out to
eat and order something you've never had before. It just
might be the boost you need!

Mind-set

Jesus replied, "What is impossible with man is possible with God."
LUKE 18:27

Turn a deaf ear to naysayers who tell you, "It can't be done."
You've got inside intelligence. Jesus has told you that, with
God, the impossible is possible! He'll equip you to do what-
ever you set your mind to. That's a great mind-set!

I can do anything through You, Lord. Watch me go!

Spa-"aah" Moment!

Try your hand at knitting or crocheting, starting out
with easy projects, like potholders or dishrags. It's a great
way to help you relax, and when the project is finished,
you'll have a wonderful feeling of accomplishment.

Crank It Up

"You will seek the LORD your God and you will find him,
if you search after him with all your heart and with all your soul."
DEUTERONOMY 4:29 ESV

God requires wholehearted efforts. If you've been looking for Him halfheartedly, crank up your seeking a notch, or two, or three. Search for Him with your entire heart and soul. When you do, you'll find Him. He's been expecting you.

Whole heart and soul in hand, Lord, I come to You.

Spa-"aah" Moment!

Take a look at your schedule. Is it too full? Perhaps you need to eliminate some things. If so, ask God what to cross off. It's better to do a few things with a whole heart than many things with a half.

Bubbles of Hope

May the God of your hope so fill you with all joy and peace in believing. . .that by the power of the Holy Spirit you may abound and be overflowing (bubbling over) with hope.
ROMANS 15:13 AMP

Your God is the God of hope. And He's just waiting to fill you up! Just come to Him in prayer. Ask, believing, for joy and peace. Next thing you know, you'll be bubbling over with great expectations!

God of hope, fill me to overflowing!

Spa-"aah" Moment!

Pick up some bottles of blow bubbles (or make your own). Then grab a bubble wand and head outside. Take joy in the simplicity of blowing bubbles and watching them float on the air!

Mountain-Moving Faith

"If you have faith and do not doubt. . .you can say to this mountain, 'Go, throw yourself into the sea,' and it will be done."
MATTHEW 21:21

With absolute faith, you can move mountains. Yes, mountains! That's some amazing power. Set yourself to believing. Keep the doubts out of your mind. And you can change the landscape of this world.

Lord, I believe in Your promise of mountain-moving faith.

Spa-"aah" Moment!

Take a trip to the mountains, or explore them from home via the Internet. Relax as you gaze at their grandeur and breathe in that mountain air. Think about Jesus' promise. You *can* move mountains! Only believe!

Determination

They were just trying to intimidate us, imagining that they could discourage us and stop the work. So I continued the work with even greater determination.
NEHEMIAH 6:9 NLT

Sometimes people stand between you and your efforts to get the job done. The same thing happened to Nehemiah when he was building the wall around Jerusalem. But he prayed to God to strengthen his hands and turned the people's discouragement into his determination.

Strengthen my hands, Lord.

Spa-"aah" Moment!

Buy yourself a squeeze ball. Not only is it a great stress reliever, but it also strengthens your hands and increases finger dexterity. When you feel discouraged, squeeze the ball and ask the Lord to strengthen your hands.

Mountain Climbing

God. . .equipped me with strength
and made my way blameless.
He made my feet like the feet of a deer
and set me secure on the heights.
PSALM 18:32–33 ESV

When you find yourself suffering from spiritual acrophobia, remember that God equips you with strength. He'll restructure your mind and spirit so that you can stand on heights and not get dizzy, giving you the confidence to climb any mountain!

God, fill me with the strength to do what needs to be done!

Spa-"aah" Moment!

Visit a lighthouse or other tall place in your area. When you reach the top, examine the vista before you. It'll give you a new outlook on the power of God and the pinnacle of your faith.

Unbeatable God

The LORD doesn't need swords or spears to save his people.
The LORD always wins his battles, and he will help us defeat you.
1 SAMUEL 17:47 CEV

God, our amazing God, cannot be defeated. It's a spiritual law. He is Master and Lord over everything and everyone. So the next time you face conflict, remember that God is unbeatable. And He's here to help you overcome the foes you face. That's a praise!

I praise You, Lord, for giving me victory!

Spa-"aah" Moment!

If you don't already know how, learn to play chess. Not only is it fun to play, but it also exercises your brain. Check it out!

Eyes Open

"The Lord is with you when you are with him.
If you really look for him, you will find him."
2 CHRONICLES 15:2 NIrV

To find God working in your life and the lives of others, all you really need to do is keep your eyes open. He's the one who brought you home safe. He's the one who provided food for a friend. So keep looking. You'll find God everywhere and right by your side.

I'm watching for You, Lord. You're amazing!

Spa-"aah" Moment!

Find out what birds are in your area. Then get some binoculars, and do some bird-watching. But watch out! It may become an irresistible hobby!

Retool and Refuel

"Give your entire attention to what God is doing right now, and don't get worked up about what may or may not happen tomorrow. God will help you deal with whatever hard things come up when the time comes."
MATTHEW 6:34 MSG

Over 85 percent of what you worry about will never happen. What a waste of power! So, instead of wringing your hands, retool and refuel by fixing your eyes on the task before you. Your energy will increase hands down!

Energize me, Lord, for the task at hand!

Spa-"aah" Moment!

Buy yourself some scented hand cream, and give your digits the treatment they deserve. Before you know it, your skin will feel smooth and supple.

Keep Cool

"Don't be afraid. Just stand still and watch the Lord rescue you today. The Egyptians you see today will never be seen again."
Exodus 14:13 NLT

The problems or people that plague you today will one day disappear from view. So keep your cool. Don't be afraid or give in to the fight-or-flight reflex. Rest assured that God is handling the situation for you. All you have to do is keep still and watch Him work.

Lord, I know You are working in this situation. Thanks for taking it off my hands!

Spa-"aah" Moment!

Buy or make yourself some disappearing ink. Then use it to write down all the things that are troubling you. As you watch your words vanish, thank God for taking your troubles into His hands!

Rev It Up!

"Stop doubting and believe."
JOHN 20:27

God knows that doubting decreases our strength. Believing revs it up. Where are you on the strength meter today? Need to be recharged? Tap into the conduit of faith by committing this simple verse to memory. You "con do it"! What a boost!

Holy Spirit, reboot my faith drive today!

Spa-"aah" Moment!

Find a hymn or worship chorus that really speaks to your heart. Then set yourself the task of memorizing the words and music. It will not only reenergize your faith but also be a comfort in times of trial.

The Heart of the Matter

*May He grant you according to your heart's desire
and fulfill all your plans.*
PSALM 20:4 AMP

If you are a woman after *God's* heart, He is moving to grant you the desires of your *own* heart. Your plans *will* be realized. Keep that promise deep in your soul, pray to God for divine aid, and expect your dreams to come true.

I know You're answering my prayers, Lord, and I praise You for it!

Spa-"aah" Moment!

How well do you know your heart and its desires? Spend some time journaling, until you reach the "heart" of the matter. Then present your dreams to God, knowing He will make them a reality.

Mind Monitor

For as he thinks within himself, so he is.
PROVERBS 23:7 NASB

Thoughts are powerful. What you believe within will appear without. Throughout your day, stop and listen to the things you're telling yourself. If those thoughts and images are negative, renew your mind with God thoughts and watch your world transform.

Help me monitor my mind, Lord, and think things pleasing to You.

Spa-"aah" Moment!

Head to the bookstore or library, and check out some good books. Then set aside time to read each day. You'll be not only reducing stress but also enhancing your smarts. That's something to be mindful of!

Spiritual Plantings

Don't be misled—you cannot mock the justice of God.
You will always harvest what you plant.
GALATIANS 6:7 NLT

One of God's spiritual laws is that you reap what you sow. Are you planting seeds of the spirit—such as love, forgiveness, and mercy? Or seeds of the flesh—hate, unforgiveness, and apathy? Work in the spirit, and you will reap God's riches—now and forever!

Lord of the harvest, help me to sow the right seeds.

Spa-"aah" Moment!

Plant some sunflower seeds. Then when your sunflowers are ready for harvest, glean the seeds for roasting, for making nut butter, or as a delicious treat for birds and or squirrels. Enjoy!

Looking Up

> "There is hope for your future, declares the LORD."
> JEREMIAH 31:17 ESV

When you find yourself in the midst of a trial, trouble, or calamity, never give up hope, never surrender to despair. Keep looking up, facing forward, knowing that ultimately God will make everything come out all right.

I don't know what the future holds, Lord, but I trust You to make things right.

Spa-"aah" Moment!

Watch the romantic, feel-good movie *Hope Floats*, and take heart in the line by the character Birdee Pruitt: "Beginnings are scary, endings are usually sad, but it's the middle that counts the most. . . . Just give hope a chance to float up."

Faith vs. Feelings

"Because of your faith, it will happen."
MATTHEW 9:29 NLT

What has the upper hand in your mind, heart, soul, and spirit—faith or feelings? If you have faith that God is able to do anything and everything, He will do it! Faith brings victory while feelings bring defeat. Go with the winning camp, and pitch your tent in faith!

Lord, I believe You are able to do anything! I have faith!

Spa-"aah" Moment!

Grab your tent and/or sleeping bag, and head for the outdoors. Spend a day or more relaxing and getting back to nature. It's a great way to give you a new appreciation of hearth and home.

Reflections

Just as water mirrors your face,
so your face mirrors your heart.
PROVERBS 27:19 MSG

Have you looked at yourself in the mirror lately? If so, do you like what you see? If not, check for a deeper source. Ask God to help you look into your heart and mind and reflect upon what you see. Work on that inner beauty, and your outer self will become simply gorgeous!

Search my heart and mind, Lord. Give me insight into my soul.

Spa-"aah" Moment!

Once you've done some inner work, head to a spa and treat yourself to a facial. You'll get not only a deep cleansing but also an improved complexion. Before you know it, you'll be glowing inside and out!

Never Fear

I fear no evil, for You are with me;
Your rod and Your staff, they comfort me.
PSALM 23:4 NASB

Your Good Shepherd is right by your side. And He's armed. He's got His rod to protect you and His staff to guide you. So even though things may look scary and dark, no need to worry or fear or run for cover. Buck up, woman! You've got *God* on your side!

Good Shepherd and Comforter, I'll never fear for You are here!

Spa-"aah" Moment!

Google *shepherd's pie* on the Internet, print out the recipe, and make it for dinner sometime this week. Shepherd's pie is great comfort food. Enjoy!

Endless Resource

The steadfast love of the LORD never ceases;
his mercies never come to an end;
they are new every morning;
great is your faithfulness.
LAMENTATIONS 3:22–23 ESV

God is so compassionate. He knows you're only human and will, at times, fail Him, yourself, or others. But God's love for you is endless. So don't give up. Tap into His fresh supply of mercy and power every morning, and walk forward in renewed hope!

Lord, pour out Your mercy upon me!

Spa-"aah" Moment!

Unlike God's love, earthly resources are not endless. This week make a point of conserving water. Doing so will not only help the earth but also lower your expenses. That's something you can bank on!

Serenity vs. Stress

God is not a God of confusion but a God of peace.
1 CORINTHIANS 14:33 NCV

When chaos and confusion are reigning in your life, serenity goes out the door, and stress moves in. Do yourself a favor. Rid your life of confusing clutter, and watch peace rain in!

I want a simpler life, Lord. Give me wisdom as I declutter!

Spa-"aah" Moment!

Spend a few hours getting rid of the things around the house that you don't really need. Then give those items to charity or have a garage sale. The end result will be an overwhelming sense of peace and perhaps a bit of extra change in your pocket!

Golden Silence

The Lord your God is in the midst of you. . . ! He will rejoice over you with joy. . .and in His love He will be silent and make no mention [of past sins, or even recall them].
ZEPHANIAH 3:17 AMP

God is watching you and knows every decision you make. But no matter what you do, He, unlike fellow humans, will never say, "I told you so!" Instead, He will rejoice over you and love you! How great He is! His silence about past sins is truly golden!

Thank You, God, for exulting over me!

Spa-"aah" Moment!

Stores now have coloring books for adults! How cool is that? Buy one for yourself, grab some crayons, and spend some time coloring inside the lines. You may be surprised how relaxing that really is!

A Faith Lift

*Though there are no sheep in the pen
and no cattle in the stalls,
yet I will rejoice in the LORD.*
HABAKKUK 3:17–18

Okay. So maybe things didn't go as you planned. Instead of wallowing in self-pity or fuming in frustration, sing praises to the Lord! Before you know it, you will have your focus where it belongs—on God—and find your faith lifting you higher and higher!

I lift my voice and rejoice in You, O Lord!

Spa-"aah" Moment!

Music can be a great mood enhancer. Give yourself some music therapy by listening to lively, uplifting tunes in the morning and calming, peaceful tunes before bed. From revival to restful, music is the key!

Constant Companion

*"I, your God, have a firm grip on you and I'm not letting go.
I'm telling you, 'Don't panic. I'm right here to help you.' "*
ISAIAH 41:13 MSG

Some people may come and go in our lives. But there is
someone who'll never desert you. His name is *Immanuel—*
"God with us"—and He will never let you go. He'll always
be there to encourage and guide, comfort and revive you.
Never fear! God is here!

Lead me, Lord. Guide me through this maze called life.

Spa-"aah" Moment!

Write an upbeat letter to an old friend. You may have the
words he or she needs right now.

Divine Inspiration

"'Call to me and I will answer you. I'll tell you marvelous and wondrous things that you could never figure out on your own.'"
JEREMIAH 33:3 MSG

When you need discernment, wisdom, or insight into a situation, God is never farther than a prayer away. He, the source of all knowledge, will give you the inside scoop. He'll tell you things you never even imagined. That's divine inspiration!

I come to You in prayer, Lord, seeking Your knowledge. Fill me up!

Spa-"aah" Moment!

This weekend, relax after church with a cup of chamomile tea and the Sunday paper. For a laugh, read the comics. Exercise your brain with the puzzle page. Fill your day with "good news"!

Lessen the Stressin'

*"Do not worry about your life, what you will eat or drink;
or about your body, what you will wear."*
MATTHEW 6:25

Keep your wardrobe simple. God doesn't want you worrying about what shoes to wear with what dress. He wants you to keep your mind on Him. He'll handle the rest.

God, help me to keep my eyes on You.

Spa-"aah" Moment!

Take a good look at your wardrobe, and get rid of the clothes you don't wear. Then make it a nightly routine to set aside what you'll wear the next morning. Doing so will give you one less thing to think about tomorrow.

Strength Training

David was greatly distressed because the men were talking of stoning him. . . . But David found strength in the LORD his God.
1 SAMUEL 30:6

It's easy to get dismayed, anxious, or frightened by what others say. When hurtful, worrisome words echo in your ears, drown them out with a prayer to the God Almighty. He will give you strength and shield you from the slings and arrows of others.

Lord, fill my mind with Your good words and my heart with Your awesome strength.

Spa-"aah" Moment!

Look around for some free gym membership offers, and give it a try. Working out increases not only your strength but also your endorphins. That's a winning combination!

Your Champion

Light, space, zest—that's GOD!
So, with him on my side I'm fearless,
afraid of no one and nothing.
PSALM 27:1 MSG

God is bigger than anything and anybody. Imagine it! There is nothing that can stand up to Him! And He's *your* champion! Be fearless! Be brave! Be confident! And, like David, you will win the victory against whatever giants you face!

You are my champion, Lord. Let's go!

Spa-"aah" Moment!

Check out a TV show or book about the planets. The grandeur of the galaxy, universe, and beyond will amaze you. And when you imagine that God is bigger than all that, you can rest easy, knowing that He's in your corner, working everything out!

God-Seeker

"Seek first God's kingdom and what God wants.
Then all your other needs will be met as well."
MATTHEW 6:33 NCV

When you trust in God's willingness, readiness, and ability to provide you with what you need, you'll no longer be preoccupied with the essentials. Then you can put your focus on what *God* wants you to do. Endeavor to seek Him first, and all the rest will fall into place.

I come seeking Your face, God, knowing You'll handle the rest!

Spa-"aah" Moment!

Get yourself some scented candles to create a warm and soothing atmosphere at home or work. Try different scents to discover which satisfies you more. It'll be a pleasure!

Wait!

Wait for the LORD;
be strong and let your heart take courage;
yes, wait for the LORD.
PSALM 27:14 NASB

Courage is framed by patience in the Lord, trust that He will bring about what He has promised in your life. *Wait,* be brave, *and wait* some more. Dig into ensured expectation that His promises will be realized and your courage will grow!

As I walk by faith, Lord, I become stronger every day!

Spa-"aah" Moment!

Write down the date, list your plans for the future, and then put them into God's hands. Later, revisit the list, and check off which plans have materialized and when or how other plans have changed. You'll soon discover that patience in the Lord *is* a virtue!

Wordwise

Help others with encouraging words;
don't drag them down by finding fault.
ROMANS 14:19 MSG

Once words leave the mouth, they can never be taken back. Their intent—for good or evil—lingers. Discouraging words leave the hearer wounded and the speaker full of latent remorse. Think before you speak. And aim for harmony. Peace, sister, peace!

Lord, I want to pass Your love on to others. Help me say the right things at the right time.

Spa-"aah" Moment!

Draw on your driveway or sidewalk with sidewalk chalk. Include words like *peace, joy, love, hope,* etc. You'll be lifting up the hearts of your readers, as well as your own!

Alone with God

Before daybreak the next morning,
Jesus got up and went out to an isolated place to pray.
MARK 1:35 NLT

Jesus, the amazing Miracle Worker, knew what to do to refuel. In the still hours of the morning, He went off by Himself to a secluded place to connect with His Father. Follow His example, and you'll find your energy and devotion increase tenfold!

Father God, I reach out for You in the stillness of this day.

Spa-"aah" Moment!

Whether you are an early bird or a night owl, find a place, within or outside of your home, where you can come to the Lord alone while everyone else is still sleeping. Journal the benefits of your experience.

Safely Home

"In the desert you saw how the LORD your God carried you, like one carries a child. And he has brought you safely all the way to this place."
DEUTERONOMY 1:31 NCV

Wondering where God is in the midst of trials? Reflect on the way God delivered you from trouble in the past. Know that He loves you and that He will carry you out of calamity again and again and again, until you're safely home.

Abba God, my arms are reaching out to You. Pick me up out of these trials.

Spa-"aah" Moment!

Treat yourself to a baseball game (minor-league tickets are more reasonable). Be sure to stand up and cheer every time a runner makes it safely home!

Winning Formula

"Observe what the LORD your God requires: Walk in obedience
to him. . .so that you may prosper in all you do."
1 KINGS 2:3

You don't have to be half Vulcan like *Star Trek*'s Mr. Spock
to know how to "live long and prosper." Just check out
God's Word. He has the formula: Do what God wants
you to do. And you'll not only expand God's kingdom but
also flourish in the process!

Show me what You want me to do, Lord. I'm hot on Your heels!

Spa-"aah" Moment!

Make some popcorn, grab some Sno-Caps, and settle
down to watch the movie *It's a Wonderful Life*. It's a feel-
good flick that brings home the idea of what true riches
really are.

In Focus

Though a host encamp against me,
my heart will not fear;
though war arise against me,
in spite of this I shall be confident.
PSALM 27:3 NASB

When the hordes come marching against you, surrounding you on every side, don't get frazzled. Doing so will give the enemy an edge, for your focus will then be on them instead of God. Keep your Rescuer, Jesus, in focus, and He'll lift you out of the fray!

Jesus, my focus is on You. I'm ready for that airlift now.

Spa-"aah" Moment!

Use some new shampoo and cream rinse with a wonderful scent you can't resist. Relax as you luxuriate in your new potions. Change can be a good thing!

A New Day

This is the day which the LORD hath made;
we will rejoice and be glad in it.
PSALM 118:24 KJV

It's a new day! A new opportunity to build on yesterday's endeavors or to make a totally brand-new start. So get your morning off on the right foot. Rejoice! Be glad! Go forth with a smile on your face, a praise song on your lips, and joy in your heart!

Lord, thank You for this marvelous day!

Spa-"aah" Moment!

Check out the song "Oh, What a Beautiful Morning" from the musical *Oklahoma!* Try singing that song as you greet the day. It'll put the joy of life in your heart!

Boomerang Effect

"Give, and you will receive. You will be given much. . . .
The way you give to others is the way God will give to you."
LUKE 6:38 NCV

Another of God's spiritual laws is that whatever you put out there will be given right back! It's the boomerang effect. When you make it your daily aim to forgive, love, and bless, God will return all those things to you—and more!

Help me to give to others, Lord, as Christ gave to me!

Spa-"aah" Moment!

Today make it your aim to bless someone else's life without expecting anything from that person in return. Then praise the Lord for His blessings and the opportunity to serve Him!

Letting Go

Forget what happened long ago!
Don't think about the past.
ISAIAH 43:18 CEV

When you keep looking behind you, at mistakes and hurts that occurred in your past, you're bound to trip up in the present. God wants you to keep your eyes open, looking to the future. He is going to do a new thing. Watch for it!

God, help me to let go of the past and focus on the future.

Spa-"aah" Moment!

Give yourself a home manicure (check the Internet for tips). It'll make your hands feel softer and look prettier, as well as remind you that even if you break a nail, you can trust it to grow back in the future—just like new!

Triple As

Then Jesus said to the centurion, "Go! Let it be done just as you believed it would." And his servant was healed at that moment.
MATTHEW 8:13

Jesus' power is *a*wesome, *a*mazing, and *a*bsolute. What you believe will come about. His power reaches into your life and changes it. Just center your prayer thoughts, and put faith behind them, *knowing* "it will be done just as you believed it would"!

Jesus, Your power amazes me. Thank You for working in my life!

Spa-"aah" Moment!

Begin a prayer journal. Write down your prayer requests and the date on one side, the answers and their date on the other. You'll be amazed at what God has done!

Pugnacious Persistence

*"But as for you, be strong and do not give up,
for your work will be rewarded."*
2 CHRONICLES 15:7

When opposition rises against you, when others say, "Give up already," heed the words of 2 Chronicles. Go to the Lord for strength to continue in your endeavors. Be diligent in your efforts. He's ready and waiting to reward you!

I'll try again, God, knowing that You are behind me!

Spa-"aah" Moment!

Google *Tom Edison*, and find out how many times he "failed" when trying to create the lightbulb. The answer may not only surprise you but also give you confidence to persist pugnaciously!

Perfect Peace

He arose and rebuked the wind and said to the sea, Hush now!
Be still (muzzled)! And. . .there was [immediately]
a great calm (a perfect peacefulness).
MARK 4:39 AMP

Think Jesus is sleeping on the job? Have you cried out to Him lately? If not, do so! Get down on your knees, and shout for help! Next thing you know, the storm will abate, and you will be calm.

The storm is too much for me, Lord! HELP!

Spa-"aah" Moment!

Your thoughts may be the perfect storm that's rocking your peace. Imagine Jesus in a boat with you, rising up and saying to your thoughts, "Hush now! Be still!" Before you know it, you'll be drifting off to perfect peace.

Guffaw with God

She is clothed with strength and dignity,
and she laughs without fear of the future.
PROVERBS 31:25 NLT

God wants you to be assured of His care, to the point of your being able to laugh at the future. He's told you that nothing can harm you. So what is there to fear? Gird yourself with His strength. Take joy in the day. And guffaw with God!

My heart is filled with joy and laughter, for You are my God!

Spa-"aah" Moment!

Humor is infectious. Find a few friends or family members to play charades or watch a funny movie with. You'll feel better and brighter afterward—as will they!

Promises

"I've said it, and I'll most certainly do it.
I've planned it, so it's as good as done."
ISAIAH 46:11 MSG

Oftentimes, people don't mean what they say. Or they mean it but somehow don't come through. But God isn't like that. What He says, He'll do. So dig into His promises. And go forth with confidence that they're as good as done!

I trust You, Lord, like no other, knowing You'll make good on Your promises to me!

Spa-"aah" Moment!

Promise yourself some "you" time. You deserve it! So schedule an appointment with yourself for a least one hour a week during which you'll do something enjoyable to *you*. And keep that promise every week!

Freely Give

Freely (without pay) you have received, freely (without charge) give.
MATTHEW 10:8 AMP

God has given you so many gifts. He gives you love and affection to keep you moving in the righteous direction. Everything you are, everything you have has been given to you by God. Trust that He'll continue to provide as you lovingly share with others.

Thank You, God, for Your precious gifts. Be with me now as I give to others.

Spa-"aah" Moment!

There are few things more satisfying than secretly giving to others. Bestow an anonymous gift on someone in your church or neighborhood. And watch her revel in her unexpected blessing!

Look Up!

The Angel of the Lord encamps around those who fear Him [who revere and worship Him with awe] and each of them He delivers.
PSALM 34:7 AMP

Feeling like you've been left out in the cold by the world at large? Look around you. The Angel of the Lord is enclosing you in His shield of protection. Why? Because You think God is awesome. When friends and family let you down, look up. The Angel has you covered!

I praise You, Lord, for Your greatness!

Spa-"aah" Moment!

Find a good praise song to memorize. Belt out your song, and feel the Angel encompass you. Your confidence will surge!

Soaring Hearts

Set your mind on the things above,
not on the things that are on earth.
COLOSSIANS 3:2 NASB

Christ has shown you the important things in life—love, faith, charity, kindness, honesty, sacrifice, mercy, forgiveness, humility—things that cannot be bought with money. Keep your mind-set on these heavenly things, and your heart will soar.

Help me keep my mind on You, Lord.

Spa-"aah" Moment!

Find a clear night, away from city lights, and look above you at the heavenly stars. As you acknowledge the vastness of God and His universe, let your prayers take flight.

Making Ready

"Before they call, I will answer;
and while they are still speaking, I will hear."
ISAIAH 65:24 NASB

God knows what you need or want before you even ask Him. He's already making provisions for you. But He won't make a move until you come to Him. That's what prayer is all about. So go, pray, ask. He's ready to come, listen, and respond.

I come to You, God. Hear my prayer.

Spa-"aah" Moment!

Pick some wildflowers, put them in jars or vases, and place them throughout your house. Isn't it great that God already provided those wildflowers for you? He's always thinking ahead!

Harmony

Let the peace that Christ gives control your thinking.
COLOSSIANS 3:15 NCV

Some days, anger, frustration, anxiety, and stress overtake the mind, leading to wrong actions. Check your mindset throughout the day. Tune out those "space" invaders, and tune into Christ's peace. Now that's harmony!

Lord, I want to be in tune with You. Let Your peace reign in my heart and mind.

Spa-"aah" Moment!

Pick out a few Bible verses that inspire you. Write them down on an index card, and work on committing them to memory. Doing so will help to keep your mind on the right things and your heart at peace.

The Eyes Have it

. . .fixing our eyes on Jesus, the pioneer and perfecter of our faith.
HEBREWS 12:2

Want to eliminate worry? Refocus. Keep your eyes on Jesus—not on circumstances (see Matthew 14:23–33); not on your own interests (see Matthew 16:13–28); not on the flesh (see Matthew 26:69–75); and not on others (see John 21:21–22). What peace!

I'm looking to You, Jesus, my anchor and mainstay.

Spa-"aah" Moment!

Spend some time outside today. If it's warm enough, take off your shoes and socks. Feel the grass under your feet, the sun on your face, the wind in your hair. Relish the time you have, and celebrate the wonders of nature.

When Faith Falters

When [Peter] saw the strong wind and the waves, he was terrified and began to sink. "Save me, Lord!" he shouted.
MATTHEW 14:30 NLT

You've finally worked up the nerve to climb out of the boat. You begin walking on the water, and everything's fine. Suddenly you take your eyes off Jesus, see the wind and waves, and your faith falters. Panic sets in! Before you know it, you're sinking. Reach out! Call Jesus! He'll save you *immediately*. That's how He works!

Help me to get my eyes back on You, Jesus.

Spa-"aah" Moment!

On a hot day, hit the nearest body of water and go swimming or wading. Relax, knowing that Jesus can save you no matter how deep the water gets.

God's Eye

Jesus said to Peter. . ."You don't care about the things of God,
but only about the things people think are important."
MATTHEW 16:23 NCV

As you evaluate situations, people, and circumstances, work to keep God's perspective in mind. Although you may not understand why something is happening, be assured that He's got everyone's best interests at heart. Who are we humans to hinder His plan?

Jesus, help me to look at things with a God's-eye point of view.

Spa-"aah" Moment!

Visit some historic sites in your area, learning about the people who once lived there. Ponder how their perspectives and lives may have changed had they been able to see into the future where you now live.

Face Up in Faith

"Before a rooster crows, you will deny Me three times."
And [Peter] went out and wept bitterly.
MATTHEW 26:75 NASB

Jesus predicted that Peter would fly from His side when the going got tough. Do you run and hide when challenges come your way? Keep your mind off the flesh. Focus on the spirit. God's peace and strength will empower you to face up to any conflict.

Help me forget the flesh and face up in faith, Lord.

Spa-"aah" Moment!

Consider what challenges your flesh is keeping you from taking on. Then ask the Holy Spirit to fill you with the peace and strength to step out in faith and meet that challenge head-on!

On Course

*Peter asked Jesus, "What about him, Lord?" Jesus replied,
"If I want him to remain alive until I return, what is that to you?
As for you, follow me."*
JOHN 21:21–22 NLT

Jesus wants us to follow Him, not stick our noses in assignments He's given to others. When the urge to being a ministry meddler strikes, turn your eyes back to Jesus before you trip up. Get back on course with the Source, and follow full force!

Jesus, I'm following right behind You—my Source, my Brother, my Guide.

Spa-"aah" Moment!

Put on some sturdy shoes, and take a hike in the woods. As you commune with nature, imagine Jesus leading you along the trail. Practice keeping Him in sight.

The Caregiver

I will take care of you.
I created you. I will carry you
and always keep you safe.
ISAIAH 46:4 CEV

Abba God is with you from the time you were conceived
to all the days beyond. He is your Caregiver, familiar with
every part of you. He will bear you up and surround you
with His protection. Rejoice in His presence; feel His love!

I praise You, my Caregiver, my God.

Spa-"aah" Moment!

Make a "thank-you" box, and set a tablet next to it. Each
day write down something you are thankful for and slip
it in the box. Doing so will keep God's gifts and blessings in the forefront of your mind and heart.

Think and Act

"[God] rescued him from all his troubles. He gave Joseph wisdom
and enabled him to gain the goodwill of Pharaoh king of Egypt."
ACTS 7:10

When you are faithfully dedicated to God, always anticipating His blessings, He will rescue you from trouble. He will give you wisdom and put you in a position of power. Think and act to please God, and He'll think and act for you.

Lord, I am Your servant. Show me Your will.

Spa-"aah" Moment!

Play some nature sounds CDs as you meditate on God's will for your life. Relax and let Him speak. Then listen, think, and act.

The Lord Ranger

For the eyes of the LORD range throughout the earth to strengthen those whose hearts are fully committed to him.
2 CHRONICLES 16:9

God is constantly on the lookout for people who will perform His will. He's roaming the earth right now. Do a heart check. Is it fully committed to Him? If so, get ready! He's going to do a marvelous work through you!

I'm awaiting orders, Lord. Speak! I am here!

Spa-"aah" Moment!

Spend some time browsing through antique stores. They are like small museums and can sometimes provide the most original wedding gift. You never know what you may find!

Peace of Speech

*Depart from evil and do good; seek, inquire for,
and crave peace and pursue (go after) it!*
PSALM 34:14 AMP

Have a word on the tip of your tongue, a word you're dying to say but know will cause another person pain? E*schew* it, then swallow it down! Ask God for help. He knows what's going on in your mind and in your listener's heart. He'll supply you with the right words.

Keep me from speaking and doing evil, Lord. I want peace!

Spa-"aah" Moment!

Buy a peace lily, either for yourself or for someone who could use some serenity in his or her life. It will serve as a lasting reminder to seek and keep the peace.

Listen!

But instantly [Jesus] spoke to them, saying,
Take courage! I AM! Stop being afraid!
MATTHEW 14:27 AMP

As soon as you cry out in fear, Jesus responds. He *immediately* tells you to "take courage." He *exists*! He is there! He will walk on water for you if that's what it takes to calm you down. Are you in fear? Open those ears! And listen. He's speaking to you!

Lord, I'm scared! Hear my cry! I need You!

Spa-"aah" Moment!

Head to the craft store, and look for a charm that reminds you of Jesus or courage. Then make yourself a simple bracelet or necklace as a reminder that He's always with you, waiting to allay your fears.

Before and Behind

You will not go out in haste,
nor. . .as fugitives;
for the LORD will go before you,
and the God of Israel will be your rear guard.
ISAIAH 52:12 NASB

God has got you *so* covered. He goes before you, leading you out at *His* pace, in *His* timing. And you don't have to keep looking behind you either. He's watching your back. So don't be beleaguered; the All-Powerful God's got you before and behind.

Cover me, Lord. I'm in the midst of You!

Spa-"aah" Moment!

Take family and/or friends bowling this week. It's lots of fun, if you've got the time to "spare."

Beneficent Bestower

"Bring the whole tithe into the storehouse. . .and see if I will not throw open the floodgates of heaven and pour out so much blessing that there will not be room enough to store it."
MALACHI 3:10

Everything you have is a gift from God. When you give back 10 percent through your tithe, He promises to give you even more! So much more that you will not be able to contain it all! No need to test Him in this. It's a fact! What providence!

Thank You, God, for Your awesome blessings!

Spa-"aah" Moment!

Tonight before you go to sleep, instead of counting one hundred sheep, try counting one hundred blessings. Praise this Beneficent Bestower of Blessings!

A Great Fish Story

[Jesus] said to them, "Cast the net on the right-hand side of the boat. . . ." So they cast, and then they were not able to haul it in because of the great number of fish.
JOHN 21:6 NASB

After following Jesus' direction, the disciples' net was bursting with 153 large fish. Does your net keep coming up empty? If so, listen for the Lord's prompting. Then follow His instructions *exactly*. Before you know it, He'll turn your failure into great success.

I need Your guidance, Jesus. Tell me what to do.

Spa-"aah" Moment!

Grab a rod, and head for the nearest fishing hole. No bites? No problem. You'll still have a relaxing day!

The Power of Faith

And He said to her, "Daughter, your faith has made you well."
MARK 5:34 NASB

When you reach out to touch the hem of Jesus, *knowing* that He can make you whole, His power immediately transmits to you. Your belief in Jesus' ability can work wonders in your life. Need a miracle? Reach out to Him today. Your faith *will* make you well!

Jesus, I fall at Your feet! Restore me in Your power!

Spa-"aah" Moment!

Take a Pilates class, or borrow exercise DVDs from the local library. Pilates is a great mind-body workout that will build up your strength and reduce stress, as well as make you more graceful and agile.

Great Faith

Jesus said to her, "Woman, you have great faith! Your request is granted." And her daughter was healed at that moment.
MATTHEW 15:28

Jesus applauds great faith. If you stick with Jesus, trust Him with your life and the lives of others, and love Him with your entire heart. He will grant your pleas on behalf of yourself and others. Woman of great faith, plead your case, and watch Jesus work!

I am a true daughter of God, Jesus. Hear my pleas!

Spa-"aah" Moment!

Decorate some blank cards and envelopes. Add a Bible verse or two. Then send the cards to fellow Christians or neighbors who are ill. Doing so will brighten their day!

Heavenly Delight

Delight yourself also in the LORD,
and He shall give you the desires of your heart.
Commit your way to the LORD,
trust also in Him,
and He shall bring it to pass.
PSALM 37:4–5 NKJV

God loves spending time with you. Hopefully, you feel the same. With such a great relationship, no wonder He wants to grant your heart's desires. Enjoy serving Him, obey Him in all you do, trust Him with your life plan, and your dreams will be realized!

I praise You, God, and trust You with my life. Let's plan!

Spa-"aah" Moment!

Take your dog (or other pet) for a walk today. When he or she pauses to sniff things out, stop and smell the roses. You'll end up with a new "leash" on life!

Caution: Construction Ahead

I am certain that God, who began the good work within you,
will continue his work until it is finally finished.
PHILIPPIANS 1:6 NLT

You are a work in progress. But take heart. Although you may not be where you want to be, you've already come a long way, lady! Be assured that God is continually working within you. And He won't stop until you're picture-perfect!

Thank You, God, for sticking with me through thick and thin!

Spa-"aah" Moment!

Buy yourself a puzzle book, or do the crosswords, word searches, or cryptograms in the daily paper. A puzzle a day will keep your mind sharp and young!

Come Away

Because. . .they did not even have a chance to eat, he said to them, "Come with me by yourselves to a quiet place and get some rest."
MARK 6:31

When you feel as if your schedule has careened out of control, take Jesus' advice. Come away with Him to a quiet place. Get some much-needed rest—with Him. That's an invitation you can't refuse!

Thank You for thinking of me, Lord. I'm ready to rest in You.

Spa-"aah" Moment!

Pack yourself a small meal, and head for the nearest park—alone. Eat slowly, then close your eyes and imagine Jesus sitting there with you. Now rest. Rest in Him.

Unfathomable

For my thoughts are not your thoughts,
neither are your ways my ways, saith the Lord.
ISAIAH 55:8 KJV

You may not understand everything that happens in your life, but God does. After all, He's the Supreme Being and knows so much more than any mere mortal ever will. He's unfathomable. Just rely on His good judgment. He has what's best for you in mind.

Lord, I don't understand it all. But thank God I don't have to!

Spa-"aah" Moment!

Take a class in something you'd like to know more about, maybe a Lifelong Learning course. And leave the conundrums in God's hands.

The Rock

Be my strong refuge,
to which I may resort continually;
You have given the commandment to save me,
for You are my rock and my fortress.
PSALM 71:3 NKJV

God isn't there to save you once in a while. He's your *continual* refuge. Minute by minute, hour by hour, day by day. Anytime you need Him, He's there. So run. Hide. Return to build up your strength. He's the Supreme Plug-In!

I'm running to You, Lord. Thanks for always being there!

Spa-"aah" Moment!

Find some fairly large rocks, and place them in a pile in your garden or on your lawn as a reminder that God is always there for you, ready to give you refuge and strength.

Balk or Abide

Naaman lost his temper. He turned on his heel saying, "I thought he'd personally come out and meet me, call on the name of GOD, wave his hand over the diseased spot, and get rid of the disease."
2 KINGS 5:11 MSG

When Naaman balked at following Elisha's instructions, he nearly missed out on God's blessing. Better to obey God's exact orders than act in accordance with tradition or your own thoughts. Balk or abide. You decide.

God, You know better than I. I'm ready to follow Your will for me.

Spa-"aah" Moment!

Find a board game you've never played before, and make a "playdate" with a friend. Make sure you follow the game's instructions. It's more fun that way!

Open Hands

*"Whatever the LORD our God takes possession
of before us, we will possess."*
JUDGES 11:24 NKJV

God has blessings out there for you. In fact, He already has them in His hands, waiting for you to take possession of them. He's made His move. Now you need to make yours. Unclench your fists, and open your hands. Make ready to receive!

I come before You with open hands, Lord. Thank You for Your blessings!

Spa-"aah" Moment!

Try your hand at learning sign language. Learning this beautiful visual form of expression will enhance your life and those of others.

Old to New

And you shall. . .clear out the old [to make room] for the new.
LEVITICUS 26:10 AMP

There are times when a once-fruitful ministry seems more like a burden than a blessing. It may be time to relinquish the old and begin a new endeavor. But, as in all things, before making that decision, ask the Lord for guidance. He'll steer you in the right direction.

Lord, give me guidance in my ministry for You.

Spa-"aah" Moment!

Take some time this week to clean out and reorganize your closet. Donate the shoes, coats, and clothes you no longer wear to a local charity. Although the process might be painful, the end result will be oddly freeing!

Tunnel to Victory

But they said...."You can't get in here!"... But David went right
ahead and captured the fortress of Zion.
2 SAMUEL 5:6–7 MSG

David disregarded the naysayers, tunneled his way into
Jerusalem, and overtook the city! Follow his lead! Ignore
the negative voices, keep alert for other choices, and if the
wall is impregnable, go through the water shaft. God will
help you find a way to conquer!

I need a plan, Lord. Show me the way to victory.

Spa-"aah" Moment!

Head to the playground, and then hit the swing set.
Swinging not only is good exercise but also helps clear
out the cobwebs in your mind, opening you up to new
ideas as you soar through the air!

Roadblocks

Just then, the LORD let Balaam see the angel standing in the road, holding a sword, and Balaam bowed down.
NUMBERS 22:31 CEV

When endeavors are begun without first seeking God's direction or approval, previously unseen obstacles may rise up in your path. Ask God to take your blinders off and earplugs out. Open yourself to God's wisdom and direction.

What's the word, Lord? Show me the right path!

Spa-"aah" Moment!

Take a bike ride. There are few things more exhilarating than coasting down a hill, the wind in your hair and bugs in your teeth! But do watch out for those roadblocks.

The Zone

Go to work in the morning and stick to it until evening without watching the clock. You never know from moment to moment how your work will turn out in the end.
ECCLESIASTES 11:6 MSG

No matter what task you undertake, get yourself into the zone. Resolve not to give in to thoughts like *What if this doesn't work out?* or *How am I ever going to manage this?* Let the Spirit take control of your heart, hands, feet, and mind. God will do the rest!

I cannot see into the future, Lord, but I trust in You.

Spa-"aah" Moment!

Time for some dark chocolate. Amazingly enough, it not only tastes great but also is rich in antioxidants! A double blessing!

Come Away

My beloved spake, and said unto me,
Rise up, my love, my fair one, and come away.
SONG OF SOLOMON 2:10 KJV

Christ loves you, wants to spend time with you, nestling you in the crook of His arm. He longs for your presence. Don't take Him for granted. Rise up daily. Run into His waiting arms. There lies peace, love, and contentment.

Thank You for all Your love, Jesus. Where would I be without You?

Spa-"aah" Moment!

Write a love letter to the earthly love of your life, reminding him of your love for him. Or send an uplifting card to someone who needs encouragement. It'll make his or her day!

Unscathed

"I see four men loose, walking in the midst of the fire; and they are not hurt, and the form of the fourth is like the Son of God."
DANIEL 3:25 NKJV

Christ is with you in all you are experiencing. If you are walking through the fire, He is in your midst. He will bring you out unscathed. You won't even smell like smoke! Just believe and Jesus will be there by your side.

Lord, I believe You are with me through fire and rain!

Spa-"aah" Moment!

Place a few candles around your tub, light them, and then give yourself a good soak. It's time to relax and revel in the knowledge that Jesus is with you in fire *and* flood!

The Mountaintop

The Lord God. . .will make me to walk [not to stand still in terror, but to walk] and make [spiritual] progress upon my high places [of trouble, suffering, or responsibility]!
HABAKKUK 3:19 AMP

When you abound in the joy of the Lord, you find you can do anything. You can scale the highest walls, swim the deepest seas, ride out the fiercest storm, and fight the fearless foe. God gives you the power. Take it and you'll make it to that mountaintop.

Lord of my strength, You are my joy.

Spa-"aah" Moment!

Splurge today. Buy yourself an ice cream treat. Take joy in its deliciousness. And thank the Lord for the myriad of delights in your life!

Spring into Action

The LORD will guide you continually,
giving you water when you are dry. . . .
You will be like a well-watered garden,
like an ever-flowing spring.
ISAIAH 58:11 NLT

God knows what you need and when you need it. But this is a two-way street. He'll provide, but you need to take. He's got the game plan, but you need to get in the huddle. He's got the water, but you have to drink. So *spring* into action! Get with God!

Replenish me, Lord. I'm ready to drink!

Spa-"aah" Moment!

Put a birdbath on your lawn. It can be a fancy one or just a shallow pan filled with water. Then enjoy watching birds splash around in their cool pool!

Commendable

"She has done what she could. . . . What this woman has done will also be spoken of in memory of her."
MARK 14:8–9 NASB

When women do what they can, with love as their motive, their actions are recognized by Jesus and stick in the memories of others. Be bold in your worship of God and service to others. Never mind what people say. You, having done what you could, will be commended.

I long to serve You, Lord, with love in my heart.

Spa-"aah" Moment!

Make a prayer shawl for someone in Hospice care, saying a prayer with each row or stitch. The joy on the recipient's face will give you pleasure beyond measure!

Lighter Days

Though I have fallen, I will rise.
Though I sit in darkness,
the Lord will be my light.
MICAH 7:8

Do not give up during the dark days of your life. Keep trusting that the Lord will raise you up after you fall. He will turn this trial into a blessing. Better and lighter days lie ahead. Continue seeking His presence, knowing He will make all things right.

Lead me out of the wilderness and into Your light, Lord.

Spa-"aah" Moment!

Tune into the lighter side of life with a comic book. Nothing brings a smile to your face like *Archie* and *Jughead* or *Garfield and Friends*.

Divine Commission

Amos answered. . . "I was neither a prophet nor the son of a prophet, but I was a shepherd, and I also took care of sycamore-fig trees."
AMOS 7:14

God uses the humblest, weakest people to do the most amazing things! When you are given a divine commission, don't assume you are underqualified. Go forth, knowing God has already equipped you with all you need to succeed.

Lord, I'm ready to do incredible things for You!

Spa-"aah" Moment!
Make a list of the spiritual gifts God has given you. Then pray, asking Him for a divine commission.

Temper, Temper

God doesn't lose his temper.
He's powerful, but it's a patient power.
NAHUM 1:3 MSG

God gets angry sometimes, but He can control His temper. That's why humans are still here. How's your temper? Are you as just in your anger with others as God is with us? Perhaps it's time to stop fuming and start forgiving. Let the loving begin!

Thank You, God, for loving me so much!

Spa-"aah" Moment!

One way to rein in anger is to count to ten (or twenty or thirty, if need be). Try using that method the next time you feel your temperature start to rise.

Good New Days

Be strong, alert, and courageous. . .and work!
For I am with you, says the Lord of hosts.
HAGGAI 2:4 AMP

When times are tough, people start to look back to the good old days. But God doesn't want you to get stuck reminiscing or wondering what could've, should've, would've been. He wants your mind and eyes looking ahead, scouting out new opportunities.

Help me to look forward, Lord, seeking good new days.

Spa-"aah" Moment!

Make a list of all the right things happening in the world today. It will improve your outlook and may give you the seeds of new ideas!

Projecting Peace

Make it your ambition. . .to live quietly and peacefully,
to mind your own affairs, and to work with your hands.
1 THESSALONIANS 4:11 AMP

Aim to live a quiet life. You can do so by tapping into
Christ's peace and minding your own business. Keep your
mouth shut and your hands occupied. Before you know
it, others will want what you have, and this kingdom of
God will grow!

Jesus, thank You for Your peace. May it spread like Sonshine!

Spa-"aah" Moment!

Find needlepoint or cross-stitch projects to work on.
Not only will they keep your hands and mind busy, but
they may also make the perfect Christmas gift!

Power Up!

Jesus answered, "Someone touched me,
because I felt power going out from me."
LUKE 8:46 CEV

When you're feeling lost in the crowd, stop. Look around for Jesus. Then, with faith in heart and hand, reach out and touch Him. He has the power to heal you and help you. Never doubt His potency. Great faith produces great blessings! Power up with Christ!

Lord, I need Your strength and healing. Power me up!

Spa-"aah" Moment!

Recharge your immune system with occasional cups of echinacea tea. It'll help ward off colds and infections. What a blessing!

God Chat

I said to myself, "Relax and rest.
GOD has showered you with blessings.
Soul, you've been rescued from death;
Eye, you've been rescued from tears;
and you, Foot, were kept from stumbling."
PSALM 116:7 MSG

Talking to yourself lately? That's okay—as long as you're feeding yourself positive, uplifting thoughts. When you assure yourself of God's blessings and instruct your mind, body, and soul to relax, it's like a healing balm. Keep up the God chat. It does you good!

Thank You, Lord, for Your healing Word.

Spa "aah" Moment!

Pick up the phone, and call a friend or two. Listen to her words, then search your heart for an uplifting response. You can change the world one word, one conversation, one person at a time!

"Son"

You shall be a blessing. Fear not, but let your hands be strong.
ZECHARIAH 8:13 AMP

God thinks you are a blessing. That's a great "atta girl" from the Almighty! Just be brave, and keep up the good work. You are going to change this world for the better. God won't let anything stand in your way!

Thanks for the encouragement, Lord. With You, I cannot fail!

Spa-"aah" Moment!

You've been doing such a great job, and you deserve some time off. Make some vacation plans—or just head to the nearest beach—and relax in the sun, wind, and waves. This is your time!

The Simple Life

Godliness with contentment is great gain. For we brought nothing
into the world, and we can take nothing out of it.
1 TIMOTHY 6:6–7

It's easy to get caught up in competing with your neighbor
for goods and service. But real joy lies in being right with
God and content with what you have. So endeavor to lead
the simple life. It'll keep you out of the rat race.

I thank You, God, for all You've blessed me with.

Spa-"aah" Moment!

Keep your life simple. Instead of buying DVDs or using
Pay Per View, check out movies from your local library,
and watch them over the weekend. You'll find it's not
only cheaper but also fun!

A Prayer Away

All praise to God, the Father of our Lord Jesus Christ.
God is our merciful Father and the source of all comfort.
2 CORINTHIANS 1:3 NLT

When you are deep in the valley of darkness, devastated by the loss of a job, loved one, or way of life, God is your comfort. And He's only a prayer away. Lift up your voice, and allow Him to enter. He will hold you until you can stand up again.

Lord, be my comfort and my strength. Put me back on my feet.

Spa-"aah" Moment!

After your shower today, wrap yourself up with some warm, fluffy, freshly washed towels, hot out of the dryer. *Mmm.* Now that's comfort!

God's Guarantees

Let us hold fast the confession of our hope without wavering,
for He who promised is faithful.
HEBREWS 10:23 NKJV

The Bible is filled with promises—guarantees from God.
All you need to do is trust that He will fulfill them. When
you do, trouble may remain, but your anxieties will disappear. That's a promise!

I walk in faith, Lord, believing in Your promises to me.

Spa-"aah" Moment!

Look through a Bible-promises book. Write down the
scriptures that speak to your heart. Spend some time
each day claiming a particular promise, and peace will
reign in your heart. It's guaranteed!

Superglued

*"I give them eternal life, and they shall never perish;
no one will snatch them out of my hand."*
JOHN 10:28

This world can be mighty dangerous. It's good to know there is one place where you're safe and sound—with God. He's superglued to you. There's no way He's letting you go. Remain calm and know that He's here to help. What a Savior!

Thank You, Jesus, for Your stick-to-itiveness! It's You and me, Lord, all the way!

Spa-"aah" Moment!

Save yourself some pain. The next time you have a torn finger- or toenail, repair it with a dab of superglue. It'll help keep things together until the nail grows long enough to trim it. Now that's a super tip!

Serving the Boss

In all the work you are doing, work the best you can.
Work as if you were doing it for the Lord, not for people.
COLOSSIANS 3:23 NCV

Taking on tasks as if Jesus were your boss will shine a whole new light on your work attitude. It will turn drudgery into delight! Recognize Christ as your Paymaster, and you'll be whistling while you work! Now that's rewarding!

Lord, I want to serve You in all that I do! Help me in my work today.

Spa-"aah" Moment!

Learn how to play bridge and/or pinochle. Then join a group that plays on a regular basis. Not only is it fun, but it will also sharpen your mind and give you a chance to witness to others!

A Work of Art

*O Lord, You are our Father; we are the clay, and You our Potter,
and we all are the work of Your hand.*
ISAIAH 64:8 AMP

God is constantly working on your shape, transforming
you hour after hour, day after day, year after year. You are
a work in progress. Make yourself pliable in His hands,
and before you know it, you'll be a beautiful work of art!

*Shape me, mold me as You see fit, Lord. I am putty in Your
hands!*

Spa-"aah" Moment!

Take a pottery class. It will not only boost your creativity and self-esteem but also give you tremendous insight
into the roles of the potter and the clay!

A Woman's World

By looking at [older women], the younger women will know how to love their husbands and children, be virtuous and pure, keep a good house, be good wives.
TITUS 2:4 MSG

When starting a marriage or family, younger women yearn for advice. Fortunately, God-inspired scripture has them covered, by instructing older women to mentor the younger! When done cheerfully, with kindness and love, everyone, including God, is honored!

Put another woman in my life, Lord, one whom I can help or ask for advice.

Spa-"aah" Moment!

Start a book discussion group for women in your church or neighborhood. It's a great way to develop new friendships as well as expand your mind.

Fightin' Words

Submit yourselves therefore to God.
Resist the devil, and he will flee from you.
JAMES 4:7 KJV

In the verse above, the word *submit* means "to line up under," as a soldier lines up behind his superiors. *Resist* means "to stand against." Them's fightin' words! Each day that you line up behind God, you can stand firm against any foe that comes your way! Forward, march!

Lord, I'm filing in right behind You. Lead me on!

Spa-"aah" Moment!

This year, take a spiritual retreat. It's a great way to infuse your spirit with more energy and gird yourself for the days ahead!

God-Provided Schedule

"Go stand at the crossroads and look around.
Ask for directions to the old road,
the tried-and-true road. Then take it.
Discover the right route for your souls."
JEREMIAH 6:16 MSG

When you're confused about which way to go, ask God for guidance. He's got an entire plan laid out just for you. To verify your course, check the ancient scriptures. Then head out on your route. Don't turn aside or look back. Your GPS (God-Provided Schedule) is infallible!

Map out my route, Lord. I'm relying on Your sense of direction!

Spa-"aah" Moment!

Open a road atlas, close your eyes, say a prayer, plant a finger on the map, and then travel to where you've pointed. As you go, continue asking God for direction, and keep your eyes peeled for amazing sights!

Concentrated Faith

He fixed his attention on them,
expecting to receive something from them.
ACTS 3:5 ESV

Faith and expectation go hand in hand. When you pray, firmly believing you will be receiving what you've asked for, miraculous things happen. Fix your attention on the God of all creation, the Doer of the impossible, and expect to be blessed!

Lord, praying in Your name releases power! I believe I'll receive!

Spa-"aah" Moment!

Make yourself some wind chimes, and then tie them to a tree branch outside. Each time you hear them play, remember that unseen forces, like God and wind, surround you.

Push On!

But [the apostles] shook off the dust from their feet against them and went to Iconium.
ACTS 13:51 AMP

When a negative experience leaves a bad taste in your mouth, spit it out and move on. Don't let your mind linger on it or become obsessed with what should've happened. Just shake it off. New and better opportunities lie just around the corner. Push on!

Help me move forward, Lord. Give me new direction!

Spa-"aah" Moment!

Use some fishing line to hang a crystal prism in a window. Then watch the sunlight create rainbows all around your room, reminding you of God's promises to you.

The New Math

Taking the five loaves and the two fish and looking up to heaven, [Jesus] gave thanks.
MARK 6:41

Don't be like the disciples, who looked only at what they didn't have. Look at what you *do* have, and give it to Jesus. He'll bless it then multiply it! And in the end, you'll not only be satisfied but also find you have more than enough! You'll go from lack to plenty!

Jesus, I bring what I have and give it to You. Do with it what You will!

Spa-"aah" Moment!

Bake two loaves of your favorite bread. Keep one for yourself, and prayerfully consider who God wants to have the extra loaf. After giving it to that special person, watch God's love multiply!

Building Belief

"Everything is possible for one who believes."
Immediately the boy's father exclaimed, "I do believe;
help me overcome my unbelief!"
MARK 9:23–24

It sounds like a paradox, but it's true. When your faith is wanting, you can cry out to God, and He'll give you the grace and power to nix your doubts. Don't wait! Build up that belief! For upon it hinges the successful working of miracles in your life!

Lord, I believe! Rid me of all doubt!

Spa-"aah" Moment!

Plant some mustard seeds in a pot. You'll end up with a useful spice as well as a reminder of how God can grow your faith from a tiny seed to a huge plant!

Higher Ground

The Lord upholds all those [of His own] who are falling and raises up all those who are bowed down. The eyes of all wait for You [looking, watching, and expecting].
PSALM 145:14–15 AMP

When you are at your lowest low, when you are falling with no hope of rising back up, God will reach down and grab hold of you. He will pull you up and set you down on higher ground. Just keep your eyes on Him. Look, watch, and expect His favor.

Lift me up on higher ground, Lord. Help me rise above these problems!

Spa-"aah" Moment!

Learn to play a musical instrument. You can begin with a simple, inexpensive, easy-to-play instrument called a recorder. It's a great way to lift your spirit and relax your soul.

Remade

So roll up your sleeves, put your mind in gear, be totally ready to receive the gift that's coming when Jesus arrives.
1 PETER 1:13 MSG

Recognizing that your future is in God gives you holy hope, determination, and confidence. When you allow Him to pull you into a life that is energetic, wise, and wholesome, all worldly troubles fade, and you are remade! That's living—to Jesus!

I want to live and work where You are, Jesus. Thank You for grabbing me up!

Spa-"aah" Moment!

Buy or make some dried flowers. Then place them strategically around your house, aiming for any corner that needs brightening. You'll be able to enjoy their beauty for many days to come.

Divine Power

His divine power has given us everything we need
for a godly life through our knowledge of him
who called us by his own glory and goodness.
2 PETER 1:3

Jesus has given you all you need to live the life He has called you to live. Reading the Word, gaining godly knowledge feeds that divine power within you. Continue to learn of Him, and you will grow closer than you ever dared dream!

Lord, I want to learn more about You. Lead me through Your Word!

Spa-"aah" Moment!

Pick up some travel magazines or brochures, and read up about faraway places. Imagine yourself walking on pristine beaches or climbing snowy mountains. It's the next best thing to actually being there—and a lot cheaper!

Love in Action

*Little children, let us not love in word or
talk but in deed and in truth.*
1 JOHN 3:18 ESV

God doesn't just want us to read or talk about living a
godly life. He wants us to get out there and live it! You
can't grow a garden unless you get up and start sowing
some seeds. So stop talking and start walking! Change
your world with love in action!

Give me the courage to live Your Word, Jesus.

Spa-"aah" Moment!

Head to a market or a place with lots of natural produce.
Buy a few items and use them to replace unwholesome
snacks or dishes. You'll feel and look better than ever!

Celebrate the Victory

You are of God. . . . He who is in you is
greater than he who is in the world.
1 JOHN 4:4 NKJV

The Spirit of God lives within you. And nothing in this world—problems, evils, losses, greed, grief, terror—is mightier than He! Plant this thought deep in your mind, and your confidence, your spirit will thrive! Celebrate this victory in Christ!

Lord, You are awesome, mighty, the greatest person in my life!

Spa-"aah" Moment!

Play some music and dance, dance, dance! Celebrate your life and God's wondrous love for you! It's a great pick-me-up any time of day or night!

Through It All

When you pass through the waters, I will be with you;
and through the rivers, they shall not overflow you.
When you walk through the fire, you shall not be burned,
nor shall the flame scorch you.
ISAIAH 43:2 NKJV

God doesn't promise that you won't have problems. But He does promise to be with you when you do. He is by your side, keeping you afloat in the flood. He'll keep you from getting burned in the fire. He is the One who will never, ever leave you. That's love!

Thank You, God, for always being by my side. I know I can count on You!

Spa-"aah" Moment!

Read up on heroes of the faith, people like Rev. Thomas A. Dorsey, who wrote "Precious Lord, Take My Hand" when his wife died in childbirth along with their child. Their dedication to God in the midst of the storm will bolster your faith!

187

Abundant Peace

Now may the Lord of peace Himself continually grant you peace in every circumstance. The Lord be with you all!
2 THESSALONIANS 3:16 NASB

One of God's greatest gifts to humankind is peace. And it is yours for the asking. In every trial and amid all life's traumas, peace will reign in your mind, body, and soul if you are abiding in Jesus. Remain in Him, and all will be well.

Lord, fill me with Your abundant, life-giving peace.

Spa-"aah" Moment!

Play some relaxing music. Then lie down and pray for peace—within your heart and in the world. Trust that God will provide!

Scripture Index